902485

378.771
WAR

19.45

Ware, Jane
An Ohio State profile

D1304296

THE BRUMBACK LIBRARY
OF VAN WERT COUNTY
VAN WERT, OHIO

AN
OHIO STATE
PROFILE

AN OHIO STATE PROFILE

A YEAR IN THE LIFE OF AMERICA'S BIGGEST CAMPUS

Jane Ware

William Morrow and Company, Inc.

New York

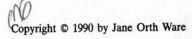

Recognizing the importance of preserving what has been written, it is the policy of William Morrow and Company, Inc., and its imprints and affiliates to have the books it publishes printed on acid-free paper, and we exert our best efforts to that end.

Library of Congress Cataloging-in-Publication Data

Ware, Jane Orth, An Ohio state profile: A year in the life of America's biggest campus / by Jane Orth Ware.
   p. cm.
  ISBN 0-688-08393-5
  1. Ohio State University—History—20th century. 2. Ohio State University—Description. I. Title. II. Title: Ohio State profile.
LD4230.W37 1990
378.771'57—dc20
                                 89-35930
                                 CIP

Printed in the United States of America

First Edition

1 2 3 4 5 6 7 8 9 10

BOOK DESIGN BY BRIAN MOLLOY

For Henry

FOREWORD

Only parts of The Ohio State University will fit in one volume; I've had to do a lot of choosing. I chose first for range: What I most wanted to do was show the scope of the place. That meant I didn't linger in one college, department, or activity, even when I could see many good possibilities. Otherwise, my selections were a matter of inclination, chance, and accessibility. And of my time frame—everything I talk about is as it was at least at some point in the September-to-September year, 1987–88, when I did most of my research. Ohio State is always in flux, though. Already, offices have moved, jobs have changed, numbers have gone up or down.

I talked to many, many people, almost all on campus. I read *The Lantern* (which I cite many times), *on Campus* (the OSU employee newspaper) and *The Chronicle of Higher Education*. I used the Ohio State libraries and others all over Columbus, including those of Capital and Franklin Universities. I consulted Ohio State histories and read some of the many books on OSU football, reread James Thurber's *Thurber Album* and Philip Roth's "Goodbye, Columbus," and so forth.

Many of those whom I talked to aren't mentioned, even though all were helpful, some especially so. Particularly, I'd

7

like to thank Jeanne Anderson, Kay Baker, Malcolm Baroway, Mary Catherine Brown, Pat Burkhart, James Chisman, David Citino, Doug Clay, Bobbi Davis-Jones, Jed Dickhaut, Bill Driehorst, Dennis Elliot, Wilma Franklin, Dan Heinlen, Jeanne Likins, Sue Mayer, Virginia Midkiff, Ray Miller, Neal Milnor, Nancy Mulholland, Kristin Mullaney, Joseph Nagy, Sue Roland, Bernard Rosen, Brian Rowley, Roger Sells, Paul Simmons, Peg Townsend, Timothy Tucker, Bill Wahl; and two friends, Jerry Dare and Stephen Sebo.

In August 1987, I met Ruth Gerstner, an editor with University Communications, who has been my official Ohio State contact ever since. I could not have written this book as it is without her help. She has provided me names, numbers, facts, and the indispensable telephone directories; she has vouched for me; she has been candid; she does not sag when I call once again. My thanks to her.

My thanks go also to John Fleischman, enthusiastic senior editor with *Ohio* Magazine. This project began when he assigned me Ohio State University as a story topic; both the book itself and the temporal theme were his idea. Were it not for his editorial ministrations, there would be no book at all.

Finally, thanks to my dad, H. W. Orth, for keeping count of chapters, and to Brendan, my husband, who *heard* it all first.

—Jane Ware
May 1989
Columbus, Ohio

CONTENTS

Introduction   11

SEPTEMBER CALENDAR   15

CHAPTER 1: *An Awesome Place to Run*   19

OCTOBER CALENDAR   33

CHAPTER 2: *Teaching Everybody Everything*   36

NOVEMBER CALENDAR   48

CHAPTER 3: *Big Games*   52

DECEMBER CALENDAR   64

CHAPTER 4: *E Pluribus OSU*   67

JANUARY CALENDAR   80

CHAPTER 5: *Money and the Pursuit of Knowledge*   83

FEBRUARY CALENDAR   95

CHAPTER 6: *Renaissance Buckeye*   98

MARCH CALENDAR   110

CHAPTER 7: *By Their Hoards Ye Shall Know Them*   113

APRIL CALENDAR   126

CHAPTER 8: *The Bee Shoot, a Sheep Named Canasta, and
            Other Job Stories*   129

MAY CALENDAR   143

CHAPTER 9: *The Top of the Chart*   147

JUNE CALENDAR   159

CHAPTER 10: *Buckeye-ism*   163

JULY CALENDAR   175

CONTENTS

CHAPTER 11: *Is "Learning as Related to Agriculture" Still Relevant?*   178

AUGUST CALENDAR   191

CHAPTER 12: *Alma Mater's Apron Strings*   196

SUMMER COMMENCEMENT: *September 1, 1988*   209

Epilogue   215

Index   216

INTRODUCTION

From the eleventh-floor windows of the Main Library, you can survey The Ohio State University. You look down on the copper and red-tile roofs of class buildings, the tops of trees, the Main Oval and its web of footpaths. To the west you can see Ohio Stadium, which seems suspended between empty tennis courts and the power plant smokestacks: During a football game, it looks like a bowlful of colored confetti, mostly red. Almost all of a typical student's campus is within a half mile of this library. With cars restricted and most buildings on a modest, four-story scale, the campus below is an agreeable place to be; it is compact and even intimate. It belies the true size of the place.

The fact is that The Ohio State University in Columbus has more students in one place than any other campus in America: 53,115 in fall 1987. To be biggest is a fine, all-American achievement. It puts Ohio State in the heady company of the Sears Tower, New York City, and the King Ranch.

Actually, it is not the biggest school—the multi-campus State University of New York and University of California far surpass it with more than 100,000 students each. The University of Minnesota's Twin Cities Campus had 62,393 students in 1987, though so many were in evening programs that full-

11

time enrollment dwindled to 36,700, compared to 47,500 full-time at OSU/Columbus. Also the Twin Cities Campus is two separate places, one in Minneapolis, one in St. Paul.

But being biggest is not something Ohio State brags about. Bigness can be so impersonal, so daunting; alumnus James Thurber described "modern Gigantic Ohio State" as a "towering and umbrageous wilderness." Bigness can also imply assembly-line education. That taints it in academia, which finds bigness suspect, not entirely respectable. The same can be said for football. Ohio State is not only a big school, it's also a big football school. But however OSU football may look from the outside, on campus it is a boon: More than anything else, football makes one school out of 53,000 students.

Great size also has benefits. For a university, it can be the source of amazing—even wondrous—scope. Ohio State encompasses nooks and crannies of knowledge (earth rotation, Ovid's *Amores,* parasitic mites); feats of management (a budget of $938.45 million, 132,610 bars of Dial soap, 8,500 courses); and people who come from and go to every place on earth (including Antarctica, where botanist Thomas Taylor collects 220-million-year-old fossils).

Even on ordinary days, such an institution will be remarkable. Here steam is not used just for heating but for sterilizing in labs; here Purchasing buys traffic cones, theater costumes, bulk nitrogen, industrial pumps, and egg cartons; here the books *Freshwater Invertebrates of the United States* and *Statistics for Business* are in the Lost and Found; here at any given moment, some place on campus is being cleaned; here departments jockey for something so ephemeral as prestige.

In the 1980s Ohio State also became academically ambitious. The feeling that this university was at last going somewhere became widespread among the faculty, who credited the president, Edward Jennings, for the momentum—at least the *feeling* of momentum. "We are an institution that is less than the sum of its parts," Jennings said. "Preeminence is within our grasp." He held that size would permit preeminence in the twenty-first century. When only the big can afford greatness, bigness becomes a virtue. At Ohio State, people love this kind of reasoning.

A university also has a moral role. Thus, even though getting from day to day might be mission enough, Ohio State assumes goals—important, serious social goals, such as improving opportunities for blacks and pulling Ohio up out of the Rust Bowl. It spent a whopping eighteen million dollars for a boiler that will not only use high-acid Ohio coal, but will use it cleanly. People expect—the university expects itself—to realize some of our noble aspirations. In that respect, it is set apart. Otherwise, the university is an abstraction of its place and time: It is us, as and where we are.

That is the big campus this book is about. This is a profile of Ohio State University during the school year that began September 1987, and ended with summer commencement September 1, 1988. This is a profile not just of students and teachers, but also of the vast citylike infrastructure, even of alumni—the *whole* Ohio State community (though not *all* of it). The scope of the place, how it gets from day to day, the *awe* of such a big institution: These are our topics.

So is the 1987–88 school year, with its September-through-August succession of months. It was (typically) both an ordinary and an extraordinary year. Throughout, the business of the university held steady: Seventeen thousand people enrolled for the first time, and ten thousand received degrees.

SEPTEMBER CALENDAR

Beginnings, 1987. On September 17, 1987, a Thursday, starting at 8:30 in the morning, Michael Curran, a bespectacled middle-aged dean in a business suit and tie, talks to a group of 194 freshmen who are entering The Ohio State University. It is a pep talk of sorts. He promises they will have a chance to study "everything under the sun and some things that aren't." He brags, "We have on this campus a new major biotechnology center. We have the only institute for welding engineering. We are installing one of the first supercomputers. Veterinary medicine has the premier large-animal clinic in the eastern half of the country. The library is the sixteenth largest research library in the country."

The students, well-scrubbed and attentive, then see a movie that starts in the stars, shows the earth from outer space, and sweeps from celestial heights to a close-up of the campus portals on High Street. The meaning is clear. Though these freshmen will spend this day on mundane chores—placement tests, class registration, obtaining their own plastic-coated OSU IDs—they should remember the ambition of this place. Moreover, they arrive at the best time of all. "Fall," says Curran, "is the most exciting quarter—it just bustles around this place." Football is one reason, but the excitement is also in them, the new students: for a university, the lifeblood.

So began fall quarter of the school year 1987–88. At OSU each quarter is an entirety. Named for the season, it starts with freshman orientation, offers ten weeks of classes followed by one week of exams, and concludes with a commencement. Furthermore, everything happens with scale. The September 17 session was the twenty-seventh of twenty-nine freshman orientations before that fall quarter; in all, 6,591 students attended. They had to attend, staffer Kelly Stinehelfer said. "That's the only way they get scheduled."

The Gentlemen Prefers Marble. The school year had an auspicious prelude when, on September 14, alumnus Leslie Wexner, founder of The Limited clothing stores, gave the university fifteen million dollars, a way-better-than-average gift. It was to supplement the ten million he'd already given for the Wexner Center for the Visual Arts, which was under construction. The extra money would go for landscaping, a library, and marble instead of granite. "Les Wexner," said Frederick G. Ruffner, Jr. of Detroit, head of the OSU campaign, "is an inspiration to anyone who loves and respects Ohio State."

Buckeye Greeks. Rush week began on Sunday, September 20. That day 896 women—mostly white freshmen—flooded onto Fifteenth Avenue, the sorority row. Divided into groups, they spent eight hours in fifteen-minute visits to seventeen predominantly white sororities where the members danced and sang about finding your niche on the big campus. During the week hundreds of the prospects lost interest—or, perhaps, stamina—while the rest visited fewer sororities for longer times until Monday, September 28. Then seventy-four women got calls saying there was no place for them in a sorority they wanted, and 520 got envelopes pledging sororal troth. At the Delta Gamma house a new pledge, Stephanie Stuart, a freshman from Akron, was overjoyed: "Once you're in a house you know the girls are your best friends for life."

Only a small minority—about one out of ten of the forty thousand undergraduates—goes Greek at Ohio State. Besides the seventeen sororities above (of which two are mostly Jewish), Ohio State has four black fraternities, four black sororities (black Greeks usually rush later in the school year), thirty-three white fraternities (three predominantly Jewish), and one Hispanic fraternity. "They all have affirmative action viewpoints," said Margaret Miller, staff coordinator for Greek Affairs. "They're only protected in their single-sex status—otherwise, anybody can join any chapter. Some chapters have integrated or multicultural membership. Some have only potential."

Arrival Time. As the beginning of fall quarter neared, cars from Illinois and Michigan, from Ohio's Portage, Lorain, Hamilton, Butler, and Wood counties clogged all the reserved parking spaces near dormitories. With campus maps on the dashboard, they delivered not only students but also stereos, suitcases, and refrigerators, rugs, plastic milk cartons, and Old Milwaukee by the case.

Class Matters. Classes began at 8 A.M. on Wednesday, September 23. Journalism found its enrollment up 20 percent over the year before; undergraduates in agriculture were down by almost 2 percent, which was a relief after a decade of sharp declines; and Engineering, with 4,347 students, was still the biggest draw on campus.

Monochrome. On Saturday, September 26, President Edward Jennings spoke to the University Senate—a body of faculty, administrators, and students who formulate academic policy. He announced an affirmative action program to reverse a decline in black enrollment. "I need only to look around this room and note that this University Senate is essentially a white organization," he said. He could have said the same of the whole campus, where blacks accounted for only 4.4 percent of the students and 1.9 percent of the faculty.

17

Fifty-Thousand-Dollar Obscenity. Some time that weekend, graffiti appeared between the forty-yard lines in Ohio Stadium. In three-foot-high spray-painted orange letters, an obscene message bloomed on the artificial turf. The clean-up cost fifty thousand dollars, but the job was finished in time for the Indiana game October 10.

CHAPTER 1

An Awesome Place to Run

The Ohio State University is an awesome place to run.

To start with the grounds: The university includes four regional campuses for undergraduates (in Marion, Newark, Lima, and Mansfield; total five-campus enrollment is 58,000); an island in Lake Erie; and, in Columbus, an airport, two golf courses, and enough worked agricultural land to qualify as the world's largest farm in the middle of a city. Two miles north of downtown, the main campus covers 1625.3983 acres west of High Street and extending beyond the Olentangy River.

Having the river in the middle of campus is handy for the Ohio State crew. Otherwise, the river is a great divide. The College of Agriculture, the laundry, west campus parking lots, the supercomputer, and nuclear reactor are on the far side of the river—too far for a quick walk. The separateness of Agriculture, particularly, is not just geographical. For example, plant scientists in Agriculture are generally not acquainted with plant scientists across the river in Biological Sciences.

Next, the buildings: The main campus has 325 buildings, including four chicken coops that house up to eight thousand birds; twenty-seven dormitories (one, Morrill Tower, houses twelve hundred students); 41,204 rooms; the 8.5-acre Larkins Hall, a six-gym, five-pool recreation facility where midwinter traffic runs to ten thousand people a day; and 325 elevators. For many years George Whicker of Physical Facilities was in charge of the elevators; to check their operation he would ride up and down. "You get some funny looks," he says, "when someone gets on and says, 'What floor?' and you say, 'Oh, it doesn't matter.'"

Then, the people: When classes started in September 1987, the full Ohio State University community gathered in Columbus—a city within a city. Besides the 53,115 students, there were 4,457 faculty, 12,807 staff, and 17,000 visitors a day (including a hundred prospective students and 845 hospital outpatients). The average day's total came to 87,379, which could have qualified OSU as the tenth largest city in Ohio except that outside of the hospital, only 10,708 people spent the night on campus. Even most students commuted to homes— some over an hour away, some very close by, like the sororities on Fifteenth Avenue—in Columbus.

Not to forget the trees: A student employee in Campus Planning, Gi-Chul Yi, walked the main campus to do a tree census. He found 250 different kinds of trees and shrubs and mapped their locations. He spotted black maples in three places, sugar maples in eleven, a rose saucer magnolia in one. Perhaps the best-known trees on campus are south of the stadium in the Buckeye Grove, where one tree honors each member of the first football team and each Ohio State All American; bronze Ohio-shaped plaques give their names. Near the hospitals is a sycamore, a putative descendant of one under which Hippocrates, the putative father of medicine, taught.

An offspring of the historic Logan Elm stands near Sullivant Hall. The parent tree, which grew near Circleville, was associated with the eighteenth-century Indian leader, James Logan. The campus Logan Elm, planted as a seedling in 1931, appeared to be developing Dutch elm disease in summer

1987. John Nagy, a horticulturist with grounds maintenance, consulted a professor on appropriate therapy (thus a branch was removed), asked a graduate student to try tissue cultures, and coveted seeds he had plucked from it in the spring.

And the nether Ohio State: The campus extends underground, where ten miles of tunnels carry pipes and pedestrians. George Whicker leads the way into a tunnel off the power plant basement. It is a brick vault, high enough to walk in but dark and shadowy, with sixty-watt bulbs every thirty feet. It's mainly a service tunnel. Pipes run along both sides of the walkway: sixteen- and twenty-inch hot water and steam pipes swathed in insulation, gas and electric lines, compressed air for labs and building control systems. Being off-limits, the tunnels are attractive to students, who occasionally find their way in and leave their beer cans behind. Whicker says the student newspaper, *The Lantern,* does a tunnel story almost every winter. That happens after the first light snowfall, when heat from tunnels below melts the snow in patterns that a reporter wonders about.

And all this—the grounds, the buildings, the people, the trees, the tunnels—all this is just the beginning: the context for the teaching and research business of the university. To do what it's expected to do, Ohio State first has to do a lot of managing. It is not unlike running a city, complete with utilities, traffic, and commerce. It is a huge job both because there's so much of everything, and also because what there is is always changing. Just in the few months between November 1987 and March 1, 1988, the number of buildings went up by two. There is so much moving going on that OSU has two vans and six full-time movers, plus supervisor Eric Esswein. These crews specialize in classroom furniture; they can stack desks with their eyes closed. They almost never move mattresses or couches but they do get lab equipment, shop tools, and pianos. Actually, in eleven years, Esswein has seen only one grand piano. A grand, he says, "eats up too much space."

Obviously, a university that measures itself to the nearest ten-thousandth of an acre is undaunted at the prospect of keeping track of itself. It knows also that its total of five square miles in Columbus are worth $239 million. It knows all of its square footage indoors and it's rewarded for knowing; the state pays a maintenance subsidy based on area.

Okey Tolley has spent twenty years in Campus Planning, where he maps Ohio State, inside and outside. He has done all the grounds and every floorplan not once, but five times, in five different scales. Drawings of the Wexner Center took him a year, on and off. ("It has a lot of weird-shaped rooms," he explains.) Three times he's walked the campus to check sidewalks, fences, light poles, and hitherto unmapped extensions of parking-lot paving.

Sometimes people make changes in buildings and forget to mention it to Campus Planning. (As Tolley says, "Every once in a while, someone tears down a wall and it slips through the cracks.") Thus periodically Tolley sends out a student employee to compare official blueprints with the actual buildings, which is what Jennifer Biechele, a senior majoring in physical education, is doing in 1988. With a clipboard full of floorplans, she is surveying almost every campus building (not the barns, for instance). One morning she is checking Robinson Laboratory, a two-story painted brick building with a red-tile roof. It houses Mechanical Engineering, so Biechele comes upon Turbomachine and Optics Labs; Gear Dynamics; a metal box the size of a house that contains a subcritical nuclear reactor; and a student running a furnace to study sulfur emissions from Ohio coal combustion.

With all the vigor you'd expect of a physical education major, Biechele trots from room to room in Robinson Laboratory: "Hi, I'm from Campus Planning. I'm just checking your doors and windows." She apologizes to the startled occupants of one office: "Just seeing if you have connecting doors." A professor pauses mid-sentence as Biechele's head appears at the door, pivots for a quick survey and then vanishes. When she asks a man at a desk if anything in his office has changed, he answers, "No. Not since 1954." And he laughs.

When Biechele does find a change, she puts it on the floorplan in red pencil. In all of Robinson Laboratory she finds only a few: two bricked-up windows, a fence enclosing a research area, a service window in a wall.

Not only does Ohio State have land and buildings, it also takes care of them, in two dimensions. The first is the here and now, served for example by five hundred concrete trash containers that two people work full time to empty. Dean Ramsey, head of Physical Facilities, tests them by walking around with a piece of rubbish in his hand: Does he come to a waste basket before he's desperate just to drop it? Ohio State also has a cleaning service. It covers nine million square feet, washes more blackboards than we ever knew there were, and, as befits a university operation, is into research: They're studying high-speed floor waxes and the bacteria kill of soaps.

Also in the here and now, Mike Davis tends grounds. He works some on the agricultural campus but he is mostly in Buckeye Village, a housing complex for students who have families. Many are foreign. Once a Moslem woman gave Davis a check for thirty dollars during Ramadan. She explained that instead of fasting, she could give money to the poor. "I tried to tell her I was not poor," Davis says. In fact, in the eyes of Buckeye Village children, he is rich. "These two- and three-year-olds follow you around," he says. "If you ride a lawnmower you're in the same class as firemen and pilots."

It happens that Davis has two degrees from Ohio State. He got the first, in science education, in 1964, and the second, in fine arts with a major in sculpture, in 1978, which was also the year he started in grounds maintenance. He always wears a blue bandana on his head. "People think it's an affectation," he says. "But I'm bald. I don't want to get burned."

Carrying a black plastic bag, he meanders through Buckeye Village pulling weeds from under the shrubs. "If this job is done well," he says, "it doesn't look like anything happened. People don't notice—when you're a student your head is full of Nietzsche or whatever. I can remember going to school here and only once seeing a man plowing snow. It's rare that we get complaints. They all come from people within our department."

Davis sometimes comes in on his own time to spray or to prune. "Pruning," he says, "is more or less artful. There are two ways of art, adding or removing stuff until it looks good. Here we prune. Mow. Pick up a gum wrapper. Grounds maintenance is art by subtractive process."

In the historic dimension, John Herrick takes care of Ohio State's buildings and grounds; in that, he has a near monopoly. Now eighty-three, Herrick retired from Campus Planning in 1967 and five years later came back as a volunteer to produce histories of campus maps and of every building ever built (even gas meter houses and traffic booths). "I went into the past," he says, "and one thing led to another."

A lanky man with a long face and a bow tie under it, John Herrick has waded through every issue of *The Lantern,* plus all the board minutes and alumni monthlies. "You have to scan rapidly to do this sort of thing," he explains. "You look for key words: *building* or the name of a building." He tracked down one thousand buildings, but there was one he never could identify, though he tried for six months. He knows it existed because it showed up in at least two pictures from the 1880s. He thinks it was a carriage house from the Neil farm, which occupied the site before the university, but he found no mention of it in all the Neil family papers, pro-bate files, or property records back to the family that sold the land to the Neils in 1827. He acknowledges that it was a minor building. "I'd have been surprised to find it."

Herrick did special studies of two campus landmarks, the Main Oval and Mirror Lake. "A lot of people assume the Oval has been here from the beginning," he says. "That is not true. It started as a lawn around the turn of the century." As early as 1901 it had an oval shape, but the name wasn't used until 1910. From 1920, it was capitalized.

Similarly, he says, there was no Mirror Lake in the begin-ning, only a stream fed by springs; the lake was developed several years after the university opened in 1873. Now Mirror Lake is a pond set picturesquely in a hollow; because of a jet fountain installed in the 1970s, its surface usually is not mir-rorlike but rippled.

On his way through issues of *The Lantern,* Herrick found that the name Mirror Lake came into use in 1909. He found also that the lake was traditionally used for the "involuntary immersion of freshmen," a practice that peaked in 1925 when 230 were dunked in May. It has been used also for sketching classes and the study of marine life (both in 1931) and for the launching by student engineers of a four-hundred-pound con-crete canoe (1972). In 1936, it was described as a favorite spot for necking ("up to 15 couples there at one time, in spite of proximity to President's House"); in 1979 a dog jumped in and attacked a duck ("Injured duck taken to Veterinary Clinic"); and in 1947, an eighty-year-old man confessed that he had been taking coins out of Mirror Lake for six years ("Sometimes kids get there first, and he gets nothing").

When you visit the Ohio State campus, you feel as though you've left Columbus and come to another place: a city within a city. On campus it is hard to park and easy to get lost. As in a city people are born here—3,368 at University Hospitals in 1987–88—and die here, in numbers the hospitals balk at disclosing. Ohio State has citylike rush hours, when four-lane Columbus highways disgorge their traffic onto two-lane campus roads; but the campus is distinct in pedestrian rush hours, which last twelve minutes and end when classes resume.

That this is a separate place is something telephone operator Joni Washington is always trying to tell callers who think Ohio State University is Lazarus department store, or Ohio University in Athens, or Holiday Inn, or Conrads or College Traditions—stores that sell OSU paraphernalia—or the Ohio State School of Cosmetology ("You have to explain that's not our school").

This school is the one with a $938 million budget that takes 114 pages to explain. Almost a third of OSU's total income comes from the state; more comes from hospital services (20 percent) than from student fees (15 percent); and 32 percent is from "other" sources, including gifts, football tickets, and research grants. The budget has to be on a scale to cover $200,000 for hauling trash and $10.6 million for electricity. The university does produce 4 percent of its own electricity; it uses that to moderate peak consumption.

This school maps its intentions with an organization chart: President Jennings and the Board of Trustees are at the top of 128 boxes (such as day care, Arts and Sciences, internal audit, WOSU radio and television stations, dentistry, cooperative extension) that encompass 12,807 employees (not counting faculty and students). These employees maintain drinking fountains and class bells, install room numbers and sheet metal, inspect radiators, and change locks. They staff machine, decorating, and furniture shops. They include artists, secretaries, editors, lab and X-ray technicians, radio dispatchers, cashiers, meatcutters, exterminators and thirteen levels of data-entry operators. There is a lot to be done.

This school, citylike, has buses that run continuously on a loop that connects the main and west campuses and the medical complex. These buses are free; sometimes non-OSU people cadge a ride to cross the campus. Altogether, the eighteen buses carry 3.3 million riders in a year, making them the sixth largest bus service in the state. Driver Joe Breunig totes the number of passengers on a log, so he always knows about how many people are on the bus at once. His record is 104 on a cold day.

The buses enter into the general traffic flow of eighty thousand vehicles a day on campus roads; the real challenges arise when many stop to park. Caleb Brunson manages Traffic and Parking. On the walls of his office he has photos of eight OSU parking ramps—Ohio State is the country's biggest non-municipal parking operation. Having spent twenty-one years in Air Force law enforcement, Brunson has a military bearing that lends authority to the explanations he is always having to make about parking. For instance, he explains that student cars turn over twice a day; faculty cars, 1.5 times. It is this turnover that allows Traffic and Parking to sell 38,000 parking permits even though there are only 24,000 spaces.

Ohio State has no fire department or jail, but it does have a fifty-one-officer police department. Because the university is not really a city, they have an identity problem. "We're constantly telling people we're police," says Deputy Chief Larry Johnson. He stresses that they all are "sworn police officers. We carry guns and enforce the Ohio Revised Code. People think of us as security guards giving parking tickets. That bothers some of our people quite a bit."

Yes, but his police force prepares to guard celebrities by training with the Theater Department. A beturbaned student will play a dignitary visiting campus with six or seven jealous wives and his sharp-looking concubine. Each time he stops he has to be protected from a staged assault. He survives, as did the

27

forty or more real-world celebrities—including Ronald Reagan, Jimmy Carter, Gerald Ford, and Richard Nixon—who have visited OSU since 1981. Unlike them, after the visit he and his entourage get a free lunch—and curious stares—at Taco Bell.

Theft is the most common crime on campus—in 1987 there were almost fifteen hundred cases, down from two thousand in 1981. In the 1980s the campus had one to four rapes a year and a total of three murders. In one of these a custodian was stabbed in a domestic dispute. "It happened during our awards banquet," says Johnson. "All of the investigations personnel had to leave. We don't have that many homicides."

For a while Johnson taught a sociology course in criminal investigation. To be in class from 8 to 9 A.M., he took an hour of vacation a day; with a week of vacation he could teach a whole quarter. He was the officer who started the department's SPIT program—Special Problems Intercept Team. The SPIT acronym "became notorious among criminals on campus," Johnson says; but the new chief wanted the name changed. He thought SIT—Surveillance Intercept Team—was more positive.

The teams analyze crime patterns and then run stakeouts. Johnson says officers often think they should go undercover. "Say, they'll throw a book bag on, ride a bike, look like a student, and wander around looking for crime. We do it sometimes, but it just doesn't pay." SPIT/SIT, however, solved some three hundred crimes. In a three-week stakeout at Larkins Hall, they arrested ten people for locker thefts. Another time, the team spent thirty nights on a roof with binoculars, watching for—and finally nabbing—a gang that was stealing IBM typewriters and PCs. In the ninety or so arrests the surveillance teams made, Johnson recalls only two students. "With students you get drunk, disorderly, peeing in the bushes."

At home, Larry Johnson is finishing his first book, a spy novel set in the Upper Peninsula of Michigan, where he worked as an undersheriff before coming to Ohio State in

1981. He finds his job provides good opportunities to cull material. The university setting is "a cornucopia of sensations and history and experiences," he says. And just being a policeman is useful: "Security people are in the same general category as service people like janitors. You're kind of like a decoration. People will do or say things as if no one was there."

Like a ravenous giant, Ohio State University procured—at the rate of $200 million in 1987. (That was way up from 1980's $75 million, mostly because of high-ticket research equipment.) In a year the giant consumed 179,831 reams of 20-pound Xerox paper, 2.2 million pairs of large vinyl gloves, 311,200 rolls of toilet paper, and 1.7 million trash-can liners. Medium black was Ohio State's most favored pen (56,238); it preferred yellow legal pads (55,967) to white (25,978). What the university scarcely needed was ball-type pull chains for sink stoppers: It used only two.

In the quintessential academic commerce, University Libraries spent $4.2 million on acquisitions. What it got were 54,000 books and 22,000 subscriptions. Forty subject specialists, most from special or departmental libraries, like Mathematics, Black Studies, or Social Work, decided what the library should acquire; they made almost half their selections by sifting through works submitted on approval. Gay Dannelly, who heads acquisitions, said Ohio State will also buy popular fiction, mysteries, and Lee Iacocca's autobiography. "Some institutions are much more selective," she said. "But this is a very populist university. Always has been."

The university also had to get rid of stuff, which accounted for Charles Jones being in charge of Surplus Materials Disposal. Some things recirculated ("The poorer departments will come to us," Jones said). Low-ticket items ended up in an unheated quonset hut, a last-resort bargain store that's open to the public an hour or two a day. It's filled with old desks standing on end (they sell for fifteen to sixty dollars), a harpsichord, used copiers, a lab oven, typewriters ("It used to be we'd have forty or fifty manual typewriters a month," Jones said. "Now we get electrics.") He sells boats, buses, and a hundred cars a year. Once, he said, "We sold six small planes to an outfit in Oklahoma. They flew in their pilots and flew them all out in formation."

Jones's office is a connoisseur's collection of surplus materials. Never mind that his furniture might look down at heel; it has *history*. He has a credenza that he thinks belonged to former President Enarson. He has a wooden desk that once was in the golf course pro shop. He has an oak coat tree and bookcase from the Ohio Penitentiary, which used to make furniture that has now become "a hot item on campus."

But that is not all. Ohio State doesn't run just on traffic, commerce, people, and money. If it weren't for computers, it might not run at all.

Computers handle payroll and personnel, library catalogue and circulation, alumni, telephones, and the billing, records, and class assignments for over fifty thousand students. Moreover, they measure enrollment, even to the three male American Indians who were full-time first-time freshmen in autumn 1987. That same fall, Ohio State initiated BRUTUS—computerized class registration by telephone. When the deadline approached, all late registrants called at once, and the system went down for two hours. It was the worst crash of the quarter—proof that sometimes even computers can be boggled at the size of the university.

But Paul Hill, who is in charge of the hardware, was not to be daunted. In less than four months he had a second Amdahl mainframe installed next to the first, so that BRUTUS could be taken in stride. "We doubled capacity," Hill said. "That's just normal growth."

The west campus computer room is so big—over twelve

thousand square feet—that it houses not only the Amdahls, but also an academic mainframe and the Cray supercomputer that arrived in summer 1987. Hill estimates ("my wild guess") that in this room there is $12.5 to $15 million worth of equipment. With hardly any people (*programs* are at work, Hill says) and the background din of cooling fans, this room is a strange place—just box after box of computers and peripherals. Enameled steel in creams and pastels, they look like nothing so much as an appliance showroom—one refrigerator or washing machine after another. Here nothing is venerable. A decade is time enough for three generations of disk drives, and none can last longer because no one will fix them anymore.

Student records, past and present, are under the aegis of James Davis of the Registrar's Office. Davis has a file of a million names—almost everyone who ever attended Ohio State and including, for example, thirty James Davises. His own record (James Clarence Davis, born 1/28/51, graduated in 1973 with a degree in education) is, he says, "archival," which means it is on a card. It's only since the mid-1980s that records have been computerized; the automatic posting of grades has only just begun. At the end of a grading period, a quarter-million grades pour into Davis's office. Until summer quarter 1987, ten clerks spent a month sticking them on individual records. Now the computer digests them overnight. This kind of modernization meant that the BRUTUS crash "left us with almost nothing to work with," Davis says. "Ten years ago all you had to worry about were the heat and the air conditioning."

Records assure certain legitimacies that Davis takes to heart. He sends out class rosters to ferret out students taking classes for which they are not registered. "If the instructor notices a student not on the roster, he should be questioning that student on why he's in the class," Davis says. "Most instructors don't feel it's their job to make sure a person belongs. They feel it's their job to teach. It's an academic-versus-administrative question. The information is sent for what we consider a righteous purpose. Why grade a kid's papers if he hasn't paid? You always have a few knuckleheads in any organization."

Davis also has to protect the honor of the OSU transcript. The FBI often used the Ohio State transcript as a prime example of a document that could be readily forged. It had several type sizes, both handwritten and stamped degrees. "Even the name of the office changed," Davis says. "It was University Registrar, Office of Records, Registrar. All of this contributed to the unprettiness of the record. Now with our computerized system, every one is the same."

Today, when the university sends out 100,000 transcripts a year, they are on forgery-proof paper, but OSU still has to be careful. "A person who wants to prove their academic accomplishments when they haven't gone to the university will use a common name and write to universities all over the country requesting transcripts," Davis says. "I had a case of a person in California who was the president of a two-year college. He claimed degrees from Ohio State. But he'd been a college president for three years. It happens all the time."

The Registrar's Office registers students, schedules courses, keeps track of grades and students. "With fifty thousand students it's a hell of a job," Davis says. "Because of computers, we're doing it with less people—from a hundred and thirty people down to a hundred in the last few years. It amazes me at times that with this many people of diverse backgrounds, liking each other at times, quarreling at others, all their moods and pressures—it amazes me that every quarter without fail we manage to do the job. A lot of people are pessimistic about the human race getting together. I'm not, when I see this office operate."

OCTOBER CALENDAR

Game Time. Before October 10's Indiana game, The Ohio State University Marching Band did their hallmark Script Ohio: While playing a piece called *Le Régiment,* they formed a long, single-file line that spelled *Ohio* in flowing script. As in handwriting, the lines crossed, but the marchers never collided.

Then the football crowd—all 90,032 of them, the fifth largest ever—was free to concentrate on Indiana's 31–10 victory, its first over the Buckeyes in thirty-six years. Afterward, Indiana fans gathered on the field and blocked out the big *O* in the middle of the Astroturf. Indiana Coach Bill Mallory, a mid-1960s assistant to former OSU Coach Woody Hayes, said his team benefitted from a trick he learned from Hayes: having an official work the practices. OSU Coach Earle Bruce, also a one-time Hayes aide, called this "the lowest point at Ohio State ever."

The bright note of the afternoon was the half-time appearance of OSU's first national champions, the legendary team of 1942. Twenty-eight men in their sixties came from Ohio cities like Mansfield, North Canton, Toledo, and from states like California, New Jersey, and Wisconsin, to line up in the rain and be cheered.

The next week, OSU dropped from nine to seventeen in the AP top-twenty poll; Indiana came on as twentieth.

Topics of the Day. On October 15, Women's Services offered a brown-bag lunch discussion on "Surviving the Lecherous Professor." After coffee and doughnuts at Smith Lab that same afternoon, Peter Goldreich from the California Institute of Technology spoke on "Helioseismology: Why Does the Sun Shake?"

Banner Revel. During the night of Sunday, October 18, police found a huge, thirty-by-fifty-foot flag stolen earlier in the evening from an American Legion post south of Columbus near Circleville. It turned up at 1:30 A.M. in the middle of a small beer party on the Oval. The flag was reported to be dirty and in poor condition.

Black Monday and the Tuesday Blues. The next day was October 19, Black Monday, when the stock market crashed and the Dow Jones industrial average plummeted by more than five hundred points. Economics Professor Stephen McCafferty told *The Lantern* a depression was unlikely, but some readers were late in getting his solace. Before they finished their rounds, the two students delivering the Tuesday morning *Lantern* were arrested. They were charged with snitching three dozen glazed doughnuts and an angel food cake from a bakery truck.

Buckeye Returns. The next weekend was homecoming. Richard Lewis, a 1969 graduate in marketing and now a comedian known for television appearances with David Letterman, arrived to be grand marshal for the parade. "The Oval in the spring, to me, is one of the greatest places," he said. "I've been a lot of places and it rivals Venice, Italy."

Another alumnus, cartoonist Milton Caniff '30, the creator of comic-strip character Steve Canyon, got the Alumni Medalist Award. And on Friday night Alpha Phi Alpha, a black fraternity, sponsored the Black Homecoming Dance, attended mostly by black students; Kaelyn Cocroft of Columbus was named Miss OSU Black Homecoming Queen. The next day before the Minnesota game, Jennifer Rose of Youngstown, a Pi Beta Phi sorority member, was named Homecoming Queen.

Rank Ranking. When *U.S. News* published a poll of university presidents that did not include Ohio State among the nation's top twenty-five schools, an OSU spokesman said, "There's nothing good about a survey of that type." That was not entirely true the following week when the next issue showed OSU as the sixteenth best graduate engineering school. This time another spokesman claimed not to be "surprised, but I think we deserve better."

News Items. In October President Jennings inaugurated the campus United Way campaign in a ceremony on the Oval; the first of the eight orientations for freshmen entering winter quarter was Thursday the twenty-second; the Registrar's Office took the championship in the fifth annual blood drive; and Ohio State's AIDS Education and Research Committee issued a facts sheet on AIDS, which noted there were eighty-eight cases in the county. To help prevent AIDS, condoms went on sale at the Ohio Union. They were displayed in a candy jar.

CHAPTER 2

Teaching Everybody Everything

"**O**kay guys." The lecture begins. Classics 222, which the teacher calls "the big mythology course," meets in Independence Hall, an auditorium with 738 upholstered seats. Six-hundred-thirty people signed up for the course at the beginning of fall quarter, but enrollment was shortly reduced to 550. "The first two quizzes are real horrors," the professor, John Davis, explains.

There's a slight stoop in Davis's shoulders; his black hair flows to his collar; he carries a microphone. The son of a Circleville lawyer, a Latinist who loves Virgil and Ovid, John Davis is telling the spawn of Ohio about Eugene O'Neill's use of the myth of Hippolytus in *Desire Under the Elms*—a tale of the consummation of Oedipal fantasies. Having over the years seen what students can do with the spellings of Greek names, Davis supplements his lecture with overhead projections of names and family trees:

"Antiope/Theseus/Phaedra."

"In both plays a father brings home a young wife from far off," he says, as hundreds of pens record his words. For thirty-five minutes, John Davis walks back and forth around the lectern, gesturing, joking, touching on Determinism, Puritanism, and "Barnyard Passion." With a finger shaking for emphasis and a triumphal grin, he concludes: "He's done what every son wants to do. He's taken his mother away from his father."

Two minutes later, Independence Hall is empty.

Ohio State's great size necessitates big classes—630 classes have more than 100 students—and Classics 222 is one of the biggest. The Classics Department launched 222 in the mid-fifties at the urging of the English Department—"Their kids were losing *The Waste Land,*" Davis says; it quickly burgeoned into the big mythology course because it met a humanities requirement without the rigors of learning a foreign language. Davis has been teaching it ever since 1969, the second year after his arrival with three fresh degrees from the University of Michigan. The class is offered three times a year, but now the faculty pass it around, and Davis takes one quarter.

"Because of that class, I'm always nominated for teaching awards, but if only ten percent nominate me, that's fifty people," Davis says. "But I'm always a bridesmaid. People who don't like large classes think we are somewhat oversimplifying, pabulumizing, adulterating. But we run a C+ median. It's *not* easy. Some departments are jealous of that course. It's awful, but the way this place is funded is warm bodies.

"I am essentially shy, but the crowds get the adrenaline going. I'm not good on eye contact, but neither was Odysseus. I have a loud voice. I've been yelling over drums all my life. I played in the band when I was in college. I love football. It's the closest thing we've got to gladiatorial games.

"Latin was quite big in the early seventies, and then it dropped down, and now it's up a hair. The ancient languages are hard and obviously *dead.* I don't like to say it. About the only practical use of Latin is papal documents. But mythology is far more practical—in an art museum, in reading Shakespeare, in music. You can't go wrong with the material. Quite often I'll use a cartoon. I had a picture of the Gorgon with her mirror. 'Oh, my,' she says. 'My first gray snake.'"

Davis has used the word *saga*—meaning a story roughly based on history, like the Trojan War—in describing mythology courses in the catalogue. People in the German Department protested; they claimed sagas are strictly Germanic. "There are constant territorial feuds," Davis says. Classics and History squabbled over Thucydides and Herodotus; Classics now teaches them as literature, but never as history. Even the Bible became a bone of contention. It is apportioned now by language: Greek, Hebrew, English.

At times in Classics 222, Davis has had problems with the lecture room, Independence Hall, which used to leak; or the sound would break down, and no one could hear the instructor. Normally he finds the worst thing about the course is the administrative end, what with five hundred of everything. "And you can't make any mistakes. You can't misstate something or give a slide on a quiz that isn't visible." He doesn't claim to remember five hundred names. His wife was once his student in Classics 222, but though she says she often asked him questions after the lecture, he didn't know her at all until she showed up later in his Ancient Epic class, which had about fifteen students.

The Ohio State University is a land-grant college: a beneficiary of the Morrill Land Grant College Act, passed by Congress in 1862. The act gave states public lands roughly proportionate to their populations (Ohio's acreage was third, after Pennsylvania and New York), to sell for the endowment of "at least one college, where the leading objects shall be, without excluding other scientific and classical studies, and including military tactics, to teach such branches of learning as are related to agriculture and the mechanic arts, in order to promote the liberal and practical education of the industrial classes in the several pursuits and professions of life."

The Morrill Act for the first time opened higher education to the working population; colleges were no longer to be the exclusive preserve of upper classes. Thus today, when President Jennings calls for student diversity, he justifies it as a fundamental mission for a land-grant college. Morrill also guarantees the place of agriculture; and in specifying "practical education," it becomes the source of ongoing pragmatism. For Ohio State, such tenets are credo.

It wasn't until 1870 that the Ohio legislature passed the Cannon Act authorizing the establishment of a single institution as the state's land-grant college. Three years later, on September 17, 1873, the Ohio Agricultural and Mechanical College opened in the middle of fields north of Columbus. The president, Edward Orton, lately of Antioch College, set up a table in front of the one still unfinished building and enrolled twenty-one men and three women in his register book. He wrote down their courses and later their grades.

Besides Orton, a geologist, six faculty members were on hand. Their subjects were chemistry, English, physics, agriculture, mathematics, and ancient languages. The agriculture teacher was Norton Townshend, who earlier that same year had been a trustee and the leading proponent of an agriculturally oriented, "narrow-gauge" institution. His proposal to drop English and ancient languages was only narrowly defeated, 8–7. By that one-vote margin Ohio State went "broad-gauge": It would be pragmatic, but not to the exclusion of liberal and classical studies. Changing the name of the place in 1878 merely underlined its broad orientation: Ohio Agricultural and Mechanical College became The Ohio State University.

Of the new name, Raimund Goerler says, "The emphasis is

on the first three letters: *t-h-e*. We take pride in being *The*. We see ourselves as foremost in Ohio and one of the foremost in the United States. If anybody is deserving of support, we are."

Goerler, who is head of University Archives, plucks the gist of the institution from its early history. Then rival institutions in the state—that is, private colleges—argued that Ohio State, having been singled out as the sole beneficiary of Morrill Act monies, should live on those alone. "It wasn't until the early 1890s that the legislature first passed the Hysell Act—an annual levy in support of the university," Goerler says. "Periodically I campaign to create a Hysell Day."

Moreover, Ohio State set out to teach everything that's worth knowing to everyone. Goerler traces this to the narrow-versus-broad-gauge controversy, which he calls "an issue as to the identity of this university. Were we to be a technical school, confined to engineering and agricultural subjects? We were greatly shaped by one of our trustees, Joseph Sullivant, who established our first [broad] curriculum. He said he wanted 'to teach all that's worth knowing.' I say, that is both our boon and our curse. It's our curse because no one has the resources really to teach all that is worth knowing.

"These features explain our size: We are *The* Ohio State University and we teach all that's worth knowing. And, early on we had women undergraduates as well as black undergraduates. To teaching everything that's worth knowing, add, to everyone. The first women undergraduates were the daughters of Professor Townshend. The president was surprised to see them attempt to enroll. They were admitted because there wasn't a policy not to admit them. Teaching to everyone is an accidental corollary."

Recently Ohio State has started to qualify the concept of everyone, to exclude people unlikely to succeed academically. It used to be that the university, imbued with its magnanimous populist ethic, admitted all high-school graduates on a first-come, first-served basis. Then it flunked up to a quarter of the freshman class.

Dr. James Mager is director of admissions. In a year his office fields 100,000 inquiries and in a day, up to five hundred phone calls. It annually processes forty thousand applications for admission—half from freshmen, half from transfers, graduate, and professional students. That's why Mager is a systems analyst. "At a small institution," he says, "the admissions director would have a background in public relations. My job is establishing systems."

Two state laws affect admissions. One limits the size of the institution. (In recent years Ohio State has exceeded its limit by several hundred—by 581 in fall 1987—for whom the state does not reimburse the university.) The other law mandates the admission of all Ohio twelfth-grade graduates. (This law applies to all state institutions, but others, such as Miami University in Oxford, Ohio, were not interpreting it as a bar to academically competitive admissions.) Every year, to accommodate its policy of admitting everyone, OSU cut off freshman applications earlier, until finally the deadline for fall 1986, was November 15, 1985.

"The high schools said this was ridiculous," Mager says. "It was difficult to motivate high-school students when the main criterion for admission was how soon you filled out your application. So, like every other institution, we set a fixed deadline, February 15." That meant evaluating applications on the basis of college preparatory curriculum and class rank. Of 17,612 twelfth-grade applicants for Columbus, OSU admitted 13,954; of those, 6,314 enrolled as freshmen in 1987. They had a mean ACT score of 21.1—up a point from ten years earlier. (Those who took the SAT had a 973 composite.) The university issued a press release to brag about 1987's freshmen: "Eighty per cent have completed a college preparatory curriculum, compared to 67 percent in 1986. And 91 percent are in the top half of their high school classes, up from 78 percent in 1986." The release did not mention that Ohio State was the last Big Ten school to have selective admission.

To teach what's worth knowing, the university offers 8,500 courses. The catalogue promises Sanskrit and Swahili but not everything—not Hindi or Ibo. Nor does Ohio State, as the state's creation, have a Department of Religion, though it confers the only degrees in welding engineering in the country.

The 6,749 bachelor's degrees awarded in 1987–88 were spread among 171 different majors. Marketing, which had 465 graduates, was the most popular; Elementary Education was second with 348. Communication had 215 and English, 108; 910 were in 14 kinds of engineering (including Aviation and Surveying); 297 were in Journalism. Majors with fewer graduates included Orchestral Instrument, 6; Botany, 5; Arabic, 3; Chinese, Fisheries Management, Poultry Science, and Medieval and Renaissance Studies, 2 each; and Labor Movement, 1. Fourteen were in Circulation Technology, which has to do with managing the artificial heart-lung machine used in open-heart surgery. Graduates do very well, says Richard Tallman, a professor. The average starting salary is over forty thousand dollars.

To assess a major in terms of starting salary after graduation has become the norm—albeit one in the Morrill tradition. Even though President Jennings says that many business executives have liberal arts backgrounds, most students opt for a pragmatic approach: What jobs, what money will their college education be good for? Colleges and departments have the answers ready. For example, a bachelor's degree from the College of Business brought a median of $22,000 in 1986–87, while a master's was worth $32,000. Engineers with bachelor's degrees were averaging $27,169, while graduates in social services (psychology and social work) made $16–$18,000.

One upshot of pragmatism is that too many OSU students want practical majors in business and engineering—for reasons less clear, too many also want journalism and architecture majors; enrollment has to be limited in all these fields. This is a paradox of size: Because it is big, Ohio State can offer 8,500 courses, but because it is big, too many people want the same courses. So many people may be required to take certain accounting or English courses that students who sign up late are closed out, at least until next quarter. Only 52 percent of all requested class schedules are fulfilled as initially submitted. In fall 1987, 203 students—.4 percent—were closed out of every class they asked for on their first try.

In 1987–88, while hundreds learned classical mythology, thousands—7,171 altogether—took freshman English, though in classes that never exceeded twenty-four. Accounting 211, introductory financial accounting, which is required for more than a dozen different majors around campus (including, say, industrial engineering and textiles), was in such demand that two megasections met both fall and winter quarters: In the fall, Richard Webster gave his lecture at 8 A.M. and repeated it at 9. Webster is an adjunct associate professor—a "fancy name for a part-time lecturer," he says. Fall quarter he coordinated seventeen teaching associates (graduate students and practicing accountants). Winter quarter his lectures were in the afternoon, which, Webster heard, conflicts with "General Hospital." Even so he turned in grades for 966 people, from Aaron to Zorman. Webster says he has his work cut out for him: "The Lord himself could not make accounting exciting."

But among 8,500 courses, many are specialized subjects taught in small classes for upperclassmen and graduate students. Sometimes, specialized topics can go on a binge. Take Romanian. "We represent eighty percent of the national enrollment," says Rodica Botoman, an associate professor. Outside Romania, "the largest program in the world after Ohio State is the Sorbonne. They have fifty students. We have about a hundred in Romanian culture and language classes." She is amazed. "America is a country of surprises."

Botoman is elegantly dressed, frail in appearance except for her strong, gesturing hands. A refugee, she left Romania with her husband and son in 1969 and in 1971 came to Columbus by way of an Austrian refugee camp and Cleveland. "We came with very little hope," she says. "We were penniless. We didn't speak the language. Even coping with freedom is not easy for someone who grew up in Communism. You're completely on your own looking for a job, for instance. Nobody provides it for you." She had been a teacher in Bucharest and hoped to resume her teaching career in French. "I thought Romanian would be of no use." That was before she tried teaching it in 1975. By now, she has been recognized in Romania for promulgating the culture; in fact, she is better known there today than she was when she was living there. She says, "Anything is possible in this country."

One of OSU's specialty departments has had a global impact. Its faculty and alumni have dominated their field on an international scale since World War II. Their work has helped determine the exact size and shape of the earth. Furthermore, the department offers a course program that's unique in the United States. It is possible to get a doctorate in geodetic science at two Canadian universities and at a number of schools in western Europe, but in this country, it is available only at Ohio State.

Geodesy—pronounced like the letter *g* followed by *odyssey*—has to do with measuring the earth. This is an abstract rather than a physical process—there's no crawling over the globe with tape measures. Rather, it uses geometrically based mathematics and extraterrestrial points—satellites, laser reflectors left on the moon by astronauts, radio signals from remote stars or quasars—and computers. In this way, geodesy can measure globally with an exactitude that tape measures could never approach. It has found that the size of the earth, the radius at the equator, is 6,378,137 meters. That, says Dr. Ivan Mueller, is accurate within two meters.

Mueller is head of OSU's Department of Geodetic Science and Surveying, which helped pioneer modern ways of measuring the earth. For example, an OSU dissertation on satellite geodesy appeared as early as 1958; Dr. Mueller's book *Introduction to Satellite Geodesy,* published in 1964, was the first on the subject.

The department's ultimate concern is mapping. They teach mapping by computers and by aerial photos. They teach both the relatively intimate mapping of surveying and the terrestrially focused geodesy, which provides the framework for large-area mapping: the reference grid of latitude and longitude.

That Americans don't know what geodesy is is a perennial problem for Mueller. "Geodesy," he says, "is confused with everything possible. Geology. Genetics. Geriatrics. In Europe every child knows what geodesy is." Mueller himself was born in Hungary. In fact, perhaps because in America geodesy is so little known, most of the department's faculty and graduate students were born in other countries.

Also, six of the nine full-time staff in geodetic science have OSU PhDs. Normally, academic departments shun hiring their own graduates. "I think they regard it like incest," says Dr. Joseph Loon, an assistant professor who specializes in mapping and is an OSU alumnus. But the department had no alternative, he says. "No other university was turning out graduates."

Geodesy does fit right in at a land-grant school: It's practical for getting a job. Brent Archinal of Dover, Ohio, originally wanted to be an astronomer, but by the time he was a sophomore at Ohio State, he had learned enough to know that there are hardly any jobs for astronomers. He found geodetic science—which at least in its celestial perspective was related to astronomy—in the course catalogue, and he ended up getting a PhD in it in 1987. He also got a job. He's at the Naval Observatory in Washington.

One thing about bigness—it has scope. It encompasses not only the immense but also the very small. The classes of John Davis are a good example. Davis, who in autumn was lecturing five hundred students on mythological incest, in spring had a class of only three people. Meeting in an appropriately small classroom—a seminar room with a window fringed with ivy— the three students in Greek 223 were translating Homer's *Odyssey* at the rate of forty lines a day. Of course, the students and the teacher all knew one another. Mary Gardner was working on a master's for teaching; Doug O'Roark was a graduate student in history; and Terry Tiburzio was a junior majoring in classics.

"And now comes the good stuff," Davis says. O'Roark translates: "Verily, leaning or falling on his back—passing out . . . The wine gushing forth from his throat—" Davis interjects: "And what else?" O'Roark: "Bits of men." Davis: "In his drunkenness he did what?" O'Roark: "He belched."

It was not for the ancients to trifle with banal excesses. The translation is from Book IX of the *Odyssey,* a passage in which the giant Cyclops Polyphemus, after dining on wine and some of Odysseus's men, belches up bits of his meal. That is just the beginning, for Odysseus's revenge follows, with nary a gory detail spared as the Greeks plunge a hot, pointed stick into Polyphemus's eye and spin it to blind him.

After class, Davis explains that Homeric Greek is hard for students, who start out learning the later Athenian Greek.

"Homeric Greek is unique," he says. "Homer is a dialect in and of himself, developed for oral poetry. It's like Beowulf would be to us, with some forms and vocabulary that don't exist anywhere else. Of course, there's always the Homeric question: Did Homer write Homer or someone else with the same name? But we shouldn't let a student out without knowing Homer.

"We start with reading the whole thing in English. Then we do selections. The first two hundred lines. All of Book Four. Famous pieces—the visit to the underworld. It takes me a half hour to prepare. Students have a much harder time." He's had his copy of the *Odyssey* in Greek since college. Its margins are filled with pencil marks which alert him to points to make in class. Red pencil for literary comment. Black for syntax.

Thus during class Davis talks about accents, tenses, similes, and the English word *adze,* a tool which he eagerly draws on the blackboard; he describes it as a "single blade curved in to smooth off a board." The three students take turns translating. Tiburzio gets the line, "But he dragged out the shaft from his eye, being greatly grieved," which draws embarrassed laughter.

NOVEMBER CALENDAR

Bird, Plane, Supermath. On November 2 the governor, Richard Celeste, and President Jennings turned out for the dedication of the Ohio Supercomputer Center, where the focus of attention looked like a fancy circular seat for a bus-station waiting room. In fact, it was a supercomputer, a Cray XMP. Two hundred times faster than an ordinary mainframe computer, the supercomputer could take on problems that its predecessors didn't have time for. "It makes the impossible task possible," said C. William McCurdy, the center's acting director.

McCurdy explained that compared to a mainframe, this machine is relatively small because its cycles are so fast (8½ nanoseconds, or billionths of a second), that information doesn't have time to travel more than eight feet, which thus becomes the greatest permissible distance between parts. The benches around the cylindrical core cover cooling equipment. "The smaller the machine, the more difficult to cool," McCurdy said. "Just on the other side of that wall are a Freon compressor the size of a Cadillac and four big water-cooling units. Outside, big fan units cool the water, which cools the Freon. The cooling is much bigger than the machine."

In fact, the supercomputer—one of the first dozen on university campuses—was in place partly because of chemistry professor McCurdy, who said he was an administrator only temporarily. "My motivation," he said, "was to do world-class research. As a scientist whose research survives or fails on large-scale computation, it became clear to me that unless I could persuade the university or the state to get this kind of computer, I would be in a backwater. I made a decision to get involved or to leave."

Now, after two years of involvement—lobbying, committees, even supercomputer shopping—McCurdy could stay. The Supercomputer Center had $7.5 million in funding from the legislature and $8.2 million from Ohio State; the Cray XMP was on the floor; and McCurdy's research was waiting. He was studying solar energy and molecules in the upper atmosphere. "You do one compound at a time," he said. For example, at the end of the month, he and his graduate students spent a week on sulfur hexafloride.

Secks in the Stax. On November 5 a Columbus television station reported dried tobacco, urine, and semen stains in the fifth-floor stacks of the Main Library; the next day OSU arranged for an outside cleaning firm to get rid of the mess. And *The Lantern* ran its front-page eye-catcher of the year: SEMEN CLEAN-UP STARTS IN LIBRARY. One university spokesman said the AIDS virus does not survive in dried fluids. Another said sexual activity in the stacks was a common problem for university libraries.

Who's in Charge Here. The Board of Trustees held its regular public meeting on November 6. In a room that has floor-to-ceiling draperies printed in an Ohio State motif of buckeye leaves and block letter Os, they sat at a U-shaped table with President Jennings and Board Secretary Madison Scott.

Seven men and two women who serve without pay, the trustees included a Toledo lawyer, a Dayton businessman, a Westfall librarian, a one-time ambassador to Austria from Cleveland, and five people from Columbus—two developers, a car dealer, a lawyer, and a public accountant. They were all well into middle age except Deborah Casto, president of a family-owned development firm in Columbus. A stylish dresser with blond hair, Casto joined the board in 1985, just ten years after she received her degree in home economics.

Money dominates the board agenda. While drinking coffee from ceramic cups with saucers, the trustees approve easements, contracts, fundraising, ventilation in autopsy rooms. At this meeting they heard a report on university investments, which were in relatively good shape following the October stock market crash.

The library issue also came up. An attempt to save fifty thousand dollars by reducing hours in six departmental libraries was provoking the fall's biggest student protest. Senior Bryan Bruder, who used the business library, collected twelve hundred signatures on a petition to extend hours. Jim Schaefer, vice-president of the Undergraduate Student Government, pointed out to the trustees that *The Lantern* had even suggested a sit-in. "On today's campus," Schaefer said, "students must be deeply concerned even to suggest a sit-in." All this elicited a response of near glee from Jennings. "We could do a lot worse," he said, "than have students concerned about libraries." A week later the hours were restored, and student Bruder expressed surprise. "I didn't think the wheel could turn that fast," he said. "It's too big a wheel."

Echoes of the Sixties. During November, *Lantern* columnists were struggling with legacies of the sixties. "Some of my favorite records were recorded before I was born," Jim Oliphant wrote. "What new cultural trends have the nineteen-eighties established? The answer, of course, is retrogression." Then Anne Marie Meyer wrote about how she had successfully abandoned her "narrow-minded [belief that] most military personnel longed for battle." She admitted, "Men in uniform have always appealed to me." And Todd Whited advocated letting the sixties remain in the past. "We can still remember it," he said, "but stop pounding it into our heads like it was the only decade that meant anything."

Twenty Out; Forty-two In. The sixties came to mind again when the Students for Peace and Disarmament picketed two CIA recruiters November 9. Twenty Ohio State students were picketers; forty-two were applicants for CIA positions at $25,000–$35,000.

Current Events. Overall, it was a busy but unexceptional November. There was a well-publicized arrest—a Medical School employee was charged with stealing and duplicating medical exams. And the OSU Poultry Science Club upped its Thanksgiving turkey sale goal to 250 birds, fifty more than the year before.

Then on November 16 President Jennings fired the football coach, Earle Bruce. The event hit the campus and Columbus like an earthquake. As Jennings said later, "My decision to dismiss the football coach created far more attention than I expected."

So Much for Geography. Geographic Awareness Week was unfortunately scheduled for that week, November 15–21. In spite of a display the Geography Department set up in Bricker Hall, geographic awareness was lost in the football hoopla.

CHAPTER 3

Big Games

Horseshoe-shaped, ten acres in area and almost one hundred feet high, built of concrete, Ohio Stadium seats 86,000 for football and has been sold out for every game for years. Tickets are so hard to get that Paul Krebs, who is in charge of selling them, keeps quiet about what he does. "Once they find out where I work, they ask for tickets," he says. "It's easier if I don't tell them."

The games played here are uncommon football games: They have forged heroes and become the stuff of legend. Given such possibilities, every game day is exciting by itself. Every time, ecstatic throngs will make the stadium sway until coffee swishes in cups. Not only football players will be on the field, but also the band—the largest brass band in America— whose members vie against each other each week for the right to play.

For Ohio State, football is the most widely shared community event, the common bond that comes as close as anything ever does to giving the campus a sense of cohesion. Beyond the campus, football provides a tie for alumni. And even beyond alumni, Ohio State football entertains the city and state; it belongs to everyone.

It's because of football that the nation recognizes the name of Ohio State University; in football, Ohio State has been at the top. Four times it has had the national championship—it has been the best team in the country. In ten out of the sixteen years, 1972–87, Ohio State was Big Ten champion or cochampion. At the end of 1987, with a .705 percentage in 906 games over ninety-eight years, it had the seventh best all-time record of any school in the country. It had played in twenty-one bowl games, including eleven Rose Bowls; five times one of its players had won the Heisman Trophy, which goes to the best in the nation.

The temple of Ohio State football, Ohio Stadium, is just east of the Olentangy River. It stands alone, looming up from a grass and asphalt plain (parking lots on game days). Inside, it has two levels of seating and a stand of bleachers at the open end of the horseshoe; the per-person allowance on the scarlet-and-gray benches is seventeen inches, for which the public pays one dollar an inch. The press box is roomier and offers a panoramic though remote perspective. An enclosed four-story appurtenance twenty-five feet deep and sixty yards long, it's at the top on the west side of the stadium.

In the thirties student dormitories—which have been co-op housing ever since—were built in the stadium's west wall. The top floor was attached to the wall first; then two more floors were added underneath, so Ripley's "Believe It Or Not" cited the dorm for being built from the top down. A sign on the Stadium's southeast wall—BEHAVIORAL SCIENCES LAB—is sometimes taken as a label for the whole place. Actually, it refers to psychology labs and offices added in the sixties. The psychologists have never exploited the potential raw material on their own turf, though Richard Klimoski, a professor in the department, says a stadium office provides a nice retreat for watching televised games on rainy days. The cheering comes in live.

Apparently in no deliberate disparagement of football, the stadium was looking shabby in fall 1987. More than six decades of patching had left the concrete walls mottled, as if with age spots. That September football did have a new $10.6 million indoor practice field, which would be named the Woody Hayes Athletic Center in honor of the former OSU coach, who had died the previous March. An indoor practice field is a big room. It has yard markers and end zones on the floor—plus OHIO STATE in immense white letters. The flooring is synthetic turf on layers of foam, asphalt, and crushed rock, all with an eight-inch slope from the center to the sides. It is meant to be just like the real field, except for the weather.

As for the stadium, it was ambitious from the beginning: Its original 66,000 seats gave it almost *five* times the capacity of the High Street field it replaced in 1922. It was the biggest one west of the Appalachians, curved like the Yale Bowl and open-ended like Harvard Stadium. In 1974 it became the first football stadium to make the National Register of Historic Places.

Also in 1974 OSU installed artificial turf, though in that it was not first—in the Big Ten, it was merely sixth. One Sunday in June, before the new turf went in, five thousand Ohio State fans came at the invitation of Coach Hayes for a free souvenir roll of the old real sod. Three paper boys on bicycles were first in line. Others who came included out-of-towners (from Cleveland, Dayton, and Baltimore, Maryland), and rich sportsman John Galbreath, a Columbus resident and owner of the Pittsburgh Pirates. One man gave Hayes a contribution, a check for $20.09. "Well I'll be doggoned," the coach said. "Our Michigan game score, twenty to nine."

Starting the next June, spring graduates were no longer sitting on the field, the center of attention at their own commencement. Because their chairs would damage the AstroTurf, they were relegated to the stands. Even so, the artificial turf had to be replaced in 1979, and swatches of the old one went on sale for prices starting at five dollars a square foot. What to do with a square foot of AstroTurf may have boggled all but the most devoted fans, and also by then Woody Hayes was no longer coach. Only one hundred people showed up the first day of the sale.

To play football in so hallowed an arena as Ohio Stadium, is not the lot of an ordinary student. These ninety-five men for whom football provides a university education have been heroes ever since they started to shave; they have been courted by middle-aged celebrity coaches; now they are singled out for some of the best food on campus at the training table in the Ohio Union. William White, a senior from Lima in his fourth year of the five that metallurgical engineering takes, a defensive back and team captain, gives three interviews a week during season. When he walks through a shopping mall, he'll hear little kids ask, "Is that William White?" Because he's been a four-year starter, millions of people have watched him in Ohio Stadium, and millions more have seen him on television. They may not know that he is nervous before every game "until that first hit." Nor would they know that every time he comes off the field, he thanks God "because I had another series and didn't get hurt."

"You have some people," he says, "that couldn't care less, but a lot of students here came for football. You've got some real fanatics. There are groupies out there—not just girls, but guys that want to be around you, to know you just because of who you are." He likes the fact that his girlfriend, who's not an OSU student, had never heard of him before they met. "She found out that I played football the next day, and that turned her off."

What bothered her—albeit temporarily—was that football players have a reputation for being dumb and insincere. Actually, William White has been one of the best students on the team, with an average just shy of a B in a demanding major.

"A lot of people," he says, "wonder what I'm doing in engineering because it's a tough curriculum. But you've got to have something to do over the next thirty or forty years." Besides, he adds, metallurgical engineering has a 100 percent placement rate.

The glory associated with Ohio State football accrues not only to the players, the coaches, and the stadium, but also to the home-game traffic system. Starting two hours before the game, 24,000 to 26,000 vehicles drive in and park; in due course they all leave at once. To clear the area in twenty to twenty-five minutes after a game is remarkable. And it has been noticed. Says David Fillhart, the University Public Safety employee who coordinates game traffic, "We get a lot of publicity when visiting schools see they don't get hung up on the way to the airport."

Actually, Fillhart says, the system is simple enough. Before the game, all streets in the area are one-way inbound; afterward, they're one-way outbound. This system, implemented by OSU, city, county, and state personnel, began in the early seventies and with perennial honing has been refined to a science. It does involve some personal sacrifice, at least for Fillhart. "I enjoy football," he says, "but can't enjoy it." During the game he's driving around checking parking lots. He knows when someone scores because he hears the crowd; but as far as he's concerned the time left in the game is more critical than the score. "If we wait too late our people get tied up and can't get to their posts," he says. The traffic system might fail.

Traffic and parking costs about $12,000 in salaries per game and brings in $100,000 for the season. The revenues are a mere pittance on the overall balance sheet, for Ohio State football is big business. It generated $8.5 million in 1987: $1.85 million from radio and television and $6.2 million from ticket sales. Football alone covered 42 percent of the Athletic Department's $20.1 million budget. Combined with men's basketball and joint revenues (such as scoreboard advertising), the share came to 62 percent. Then when Athletic Department contributions—many inspired by football—were also added, basketball and, overwhelmingly, football accounted for 85 percent of the budget. What all this paid for were the marching band ($94,630), cheerleaders ($15,850), 31 varsity sports—an unusually large number—and 309 athletic scholarships. Of those, 112 went to women; they included 16 in track and 2 in fencing. Of the 197 for men, 95 were in football; 1 in volleyball.

The problem with football is that for a school, the glories are treacherous. The academic world is quick to dismiss an institution that seems preoccupied with sport and wants too much to win. Particularly for a school as hungry for academic repute as Ohio State has been lately, to look like "Jock U" is to look absurd. That happened—no doubt by accident—when President Jennings dismissed Coach Bruce.

Earle Bruce came to Ohio State three times. The first time, a star high-school halfback recruited from Cumberland, Maryland, in the late 1940s, he came because of Ohio Stadium. "To be honest," he says, "it was the biggest football stadium I saw." Although Bruce later injured his knee and never did play, Woody Hayes enlisted him as a student assistant coach and he graduated in 1953. The second time Bruce came to Ohio State, after thirteen years in high-school coaching, he'd been hired as an assistant to Hayes. And the third time, after six years as coach at Iowa State, he came for the head job at Ohio State. *Hayes's* job.

Following Hayes was always Bruce's worst problem at Ohio State, for on campus Hayes was not just a football coach but a legend. Woody Hayes did care too much about winning. ("Without winning," he said, "there is no civilization.") He also visited children in the hospital; he helped with charity fund-raising; he was a devotee of Ralph Waldo Emerson. But at the end of the 1978 season Hayes, never a man wanting in passion, slugged an opposition player who had just scored. The university lost little time in firing him, even though he'd been head coach for twenty-eight years, even though he was the most famous (or notorious) person on campus. The university took a lot of flack from die-hard fans, over the firing of Woody Hayes. It was the target also of critics who said Hayes should have been restrained long before.

Bruce had a good record at Ohio State (a better one overall than Hayes); at 75–22 for 1979–86, he was the best in the Big Ten. Every year the Buckeyes went to a bowl game. After Bruce's first season, 1979, he was named College Football Coach of the Year; the team that year—basically a Hayes team—finished with an 11–1 record. The loss was to Southern California in the Rose Bowl, where the final score was 17–16. By that one point, Ohio State missed a national championship, and some fans never forgave Earle Bruce.

Bruce's critics focused on his style: The man just wasn't slick away from the sidelines. By 1987 people had been complaining for nine seasons that he was colorless, inept, out-of-date. He seemed distracted at press conferences, less than eager for public appearances. He was pudgy, fifty-seven, and had tried to spruce himself up by wearing a fedora to games. Now, he was in the second year of a three-year contract—a contract that permitted his dismissal for any reason. The lackluster 1987 season provided, if not a reason, at least a window of opportunity to get rid of a coach who had almost no admirers beyond the team and Athletic Director Rick Bay.

On November 14, the Buckeyes lost to Iowa in the last thirty seconds of play, 29–27. It was the third consecutive loss, the fourth of the season; only one game, with arch-rival Michigan, remained to be played. The day after the Iowa loss, the Columbus *Dispatch* stoked the rumors about Bruce's job insecurity and reported the OSU Board of Trustees had informally agreed not to keep him. On Monday, at his usual luncheon press conference, Bruce said, "I'm a loyal employee of the university. I'm staying at Ohio State."

But in fact, Jennings had that morning decided to let him go. At 1:30 Jennings told Rick Bay of his decision. Bay resigned in protest; he'd been reaffirming the university's faith in Bruce for weeks. The previous January, Bruce might well have accepted a job offer from the University of Arizona if Bay hadn't encouraged him to stay at Ohio State.

Jennings intended to delay any public announcement until after the Michigan game, but once he told Bay, he lost control over the timing. Bay told Jennings the news would get out anyway, so he'd go ahead with an immediate announcement. So after he'd broken the news to Bruce, Bay held a press conference at 4:30 that afternoon and told the world. He read a statement from Jennings: "Earle Bruce has been relieved of his duties as head football coach at The Ohio State University. I will recommend to the Board of Trustees that the university fulfill the financial terms of his contract." Jennings's statement also said he regretted Bay's resignation and named an aide, Jim Jones, as athletic director.

Jennings himself wasn't in the room for this press conference. There was only Rick Bay saying Jennings told him "he was under pressure to make a coaching change." There was only Rick Bay saying that "football and basketball and all major college athletics are out of perspective." There was Rick Bay agreeing that this firing gave a sad view of the university infrastructure, adding that he wasn't sure if he wanted to stay in the business. "It's a dark day for Ohio State," he said. "I have loved being here. It's a great institution."

In Bay's eyes skewed values were running amok at Ohio State. When he shared that view with the national press, it became a dark day indeed for the university—Ohio State has probably never looked so bad as it did during that press conference. It seemed that at this university, nothing was more important than winning games.

That night the OSU band went to Bruce's house and played for the coach and his wife while they cried. Everyone cried. It was the moment in time when Earle Bruce's stature most nearly approached Woody Hayes's.

The next morning, Ed Jennings, who was being accused of buckling in to big-money OSU donors, held his own press conference. He said the decision to let the coach go was his and, because he couldn't discuss personnel issues, he couldn't divulge his reasons. For better (no remarks survived to haunt him afterward) and worse (a little information might have gone a long way), he never did say much.

The trustees backed him up. One, Toledo attorney John Barone, said the pressure to fire the coach had been relentless: "Friend upon friend or call upon call, it was 'When are you going to do something about this?'" Another, Leonard Immke of Len Immke Buick in Columbus, added that the football program seemed "to be skidding downhill." And referring to the basketball coach hired in 1986, Trustee Hamilton J. Teaford, a Columbus lawyer, said, "We want another Gary Williams. He has great public presence."

Several university spokesmen said Bruce had an "image" problem—one anonymously told the Cleveland *Plain Dealer* that Bruce was "whiny, grumpy, greedy." Even Rick Bay said, "He's not Mr. Charisma." Every possible explanation was hauled out. People remembered that just before the season began OSU's All-American starter Cris Carter had been ruled ineligible for taking money from an agent. Bruce had wanted to appeal the Carter ruling but Jennings and Bay overruled him. Or perhaps—as even Ohio governor Celeste suggested—Bruce had mishandled the gambling problems of former quarterback Art Schlichter—but that was *so* long ago, in 1981. On the other hand, Woody Hayes's death was recent. Bruce was an old Hayes protégé. Maybe Ohio State just hadn't dared to fire him so long as Hayes and the prospect of his wrath were around.

Mail—almost all of it critical—swamped Jennings's office in record volume. During the week *The Lantern* published twenty pro-Bruce letters and three pro-Jennings, plus an editorial that called the firing "by far President Jennings' most foolish decision to date." On Tuesday Kappa Sigma fraternity men stood outside their house and chanted, "No Bruce, No School" for an hour. "Most of us went to classes anyway," fraternity president Gary Price said. "This isn't the radical sixties." Two days later a hospital staffer organized a pro-Bruce rally that drew three hundred people. On Friday *Lantern* sportswriter Jean-Jacques Taylor wrote, "In the span of four days, Earle Bruce has gone from one of the most maligned coaches in Ohio State history to one of the greatest ever to stalk a sideline." Students were so distracted by the controversy that only a hundred went to the annual beat-Michigan pep rally.

On Saturday Bruce had the satisfaction of a 23–20 triumph over Michigan. Still riding high on public sympathy, he revealed his $7.4 million slander and breach-of-contract lawsuit against Jennings and the university. The suit, which sought five million dollars from Jennings personally, said Bruce was fired because he didn't "approve" of Jennings's private life. Said Bruce self-righteously, "When a man judges me he ought to stand high as far as his honesty and his moral character." Bruce's lawyer, John Zonak, elaborated by charging Jennings with "carousing and excessive drinking."

Three women were subpoenaed in connection with the suit. Jennings's wife, from whom he had been separated earlier in the year, and Barbara Real, an OSU development staffer, were asked to provide financial records. Trustee Deborah

Casto was asked for board records. Real, who'd recently been divorced, and Jennings had hoped to leave together that week for a quiet Thanksgiving trip to London. When they found their vacation plans on the front page, Real changed the TWA reservation from two seats to one for herself.

Trustee Casto, who had talked comfortably with the press the week before, this week found herself mentioned in a lawsuit and recuperating at home with a broken arm from a car accident. Advised by her attorney not to discuss the case, she tearfully told a Columbus *Dispatch* reporter, "You try to do something for free and look what happens."

The university hired local attorney John Elam, who went after a settlement as if it were an end zone. He was probably helped by Bruce's growing realization that his lawsuit might be hurting the university he loved, but anyway Elam had an agreement by Friday, the day after Thanksgiving. The university agreed to pay Bruce $471,000, which included salary and benefits he'd have gotten under his contract, retirement buyout and a settlement of $119,184. Both Jennings and Bruce issued statements of regret and agreed not to discuss the case. Which was perhaps as well. Except for Attorney Elam and perhaps the beleaguered Deborah Casto, it was a story without heroes.

"What's astonishing is that even nationally it got all that publicity." So David Frantz, a humanities dean, said afterward. He went on, "You can't pretend the timing wasn't a serious mistake. Three days *after* the last game four coaches were fired, including a guy at North Carolina who'd been very successful and had five years left on a nine-year contract." Those dismissals drew relatively little notice. Perhaps the enormity of the blow-up had to do with the nature of a large, public university. "I don't think at a large state institution you could do away with intercollegiate athletics," Frantz said. "So many people identify with it."

There was another thing about Ohio State's being a large, public university. It had the momentum to carry on.

Jennings emerged bent but unbroken. Even in the national press he had suffered a general lambasting for appearing to endorse a winning-is-everything policy. His private life had gone public. But afterward, the Faculty Council voted thirty-nine to eleven to support him. After all, he had been leading Ohio State to greatness before this Jock U slip-up. In his seventh year in office, he pointed out he had the second-longest tenure of any president in the Big Ten. During the winter, he spent a lot of time affirming that he intended to stay in his job.

Within a month of the firing, 250 university contributors withdrew their pledges because of it. The amount lost was $20,000, compared to $3.6 million received that November in pledges, though a Columbus industrialist withdrew an offer to give $400,000 for athletics, which was more noticeable. Two professors of social work led a campus coalition that threatened to urge black athletes to boycott Ohio State if the university didn't appoint a black coach as Bruce's successor. And for the first time in years, Ohio State didn't play in a bowl; it turned down an invitation from the Sun Bowl.

The controversy left the campus exhausted by its excesses. Before long the "Save Earle" T-shirts disappeared into drawers. Star freshman tailback Carlos Snow affirmed, "I am a Buckeye. I'm going to remain a Buckeye." Journalism professor Llyle Barker offered a PR post-mortem: "It should have been handled quickly," he said, "with what we teach in public relations—maximum disclosure, minimum delay." Another professor recalled the publicity when Woody Hayes was fired and lamented that this kind of "embarrassment as an educational institution" appeared to be cyclical. And while some of the pundits of academia said the whole episode represented the triumph of athletics over the scholarly, others concluded just the opposite.

DECEMBER CALENDAR

Your Land Is My View. Just to the west of Ohio State, suburban Upper Arlington residents enjoyed living across the street from university farms. Now OSU planned to lease some of the farmland for a state computer center, and the neighbors were alarmed. "Naturally," said one of them to the OSU trustees on December 4, "we hate to see the loss of open space, with its panoramic view of the Olentangy River Valley." Dr. Medard Lutmerding went on to urge the university to make sure any new development had "a campus environment equal at least to the Oval."

Spoken and Unspoken. The next morning, a Saturday, the University Senate assembled at nine o'clock for their monthly meeting. In an hour and a half, they heard reports from committees (including Steering, Traffic, and Bookstores); a speech by Provost Myles Brand (who said, "Ohio State has the capacity to be among the five best public universities in this country and the best in the Big Ten by the turn of the century"); and no mention at all of Earle Bruce.

Sales. Also that Saturday the OSU Forestry Forum, a student organization, ran its 106th annual Christmas tree sale, in the Horticulture Barn. That night the Student Art Exhibition Council sponsored an auction of art works that could be holiday gifts; prices ranged from five to a hundred dollars.

Fall Commencement. Fall quarter came full circle with the university's 302nd commencement on the morning of Friday, December 11. The last class of 1987 heard speaker Henry Ponder, president of Fisk University and himself the holder of a PhD from OSU. "Twenty-six years ago," he said, "I was sitting where you are now sitting." Then he promised a speech full of "lofty statements" and delivered.

A few graduating football players wore "Earle" headbands under their mortarboards, but that furor seemed remote, though not forgotten. Other graduates carried balloons or wore signs: I MADE IT! or C'EST FINI or THINK GLOBALLY. GIVE KAZOOS TO CHINA TOO! In the audience, a homemaker and retired plant manager from Urbana, Sylvia and Edward Zelinski, watched as Susan, their youngest child, filed up to receive her diploma. The Zelinskis have seven children, and Susan was the sixth to receive a degree. Her parents glowed with pride.

No, Thank You. Having fired its coach (his record was 4–17–1), the University of Kansas offered the job to Earle Bruce, who turned it down. Another turndown came from OSU police Chief Peter Herdt. He declined an offer from B'nai B'rith, a Jewish organization, to provide sandwich fixings and soft drinks for personnel on duty Christmas Eve. Herdt said the police had an absolute rule against accepting gratuities.

New Football Coach. On December 30, Ohio State announced it had a new football coach. He was John Cooper, whose Arizona State team that day defeated Air Force 33–28 in the Freedom Bowl in Anaheim, California. At night Cooper flew to Columbus, and late the next morning he was on deck for a press conference in the 133-seat auditorium in the Woody Hayes Athletic Center. President Jennings came. So did Edmund Redman, chairman of the Board of Trustees, and a throng of reporters and cameramen.

Julie Bonfini, secretary to the football coach, was also there, sitting on the far right in the sixth row. Bonfini had worked for Earle Bruce for eight years and really liked him. But she knew, of course, that other Division I football secretaries have had more than one boss—in twenty-five years one of them had worked for six coaches.

So Bonfini went to watch the press conference, to check out her new boss before they met face-to-face. "He was," she said later, "in his proudest, happiest moment. He talked about Woody Hayes and the Ohio State tradition. The press put pointed but not jagged questions. I watched where he looked—if you watch where a speaker looks and who he looks at when he makes a point, you can get a feel for him. [John Cooper] looked at the person who asked the question. He had good eye contact." She came away cautiously optimistic.

CHAPTER 4

E Pluribus OSU

Geoffrey Young was a twenty-five-year-old graduate student working on a doctorate in clinical psychology. This entitled him to share an office, a small, austere, and windowless room in the inner reaches of Townshend Hall. He sat at his desk there, his long, six-foot two-inch frame clad in a warm-up suit, and talked about the rigors of graduate school. His whole future depended on passing his generals—a set of comprehensive exams he would take in a few months. Ever since he arrived to start his graduate work in 1984—almost four years ago—he'd dreaded these exams.

So he was studying. He had to know some eighty books and articles; this summer, he'd spend almost every morning, afternoon, and evening on them, six and seven days a week. It reminded him of his first year as a graduate student, when he studied eight hours every day while taking an onerous eighteen- and nineteen-hour course load. "They bring you in, load you up, and you try to stay above water," he said. "Nothing is really ideal in graduate school. There's always a hurdle, a pressure that never stops."

Geoff Young was from Somerset, New Jersey. His father was a psychiatric social worker on the faculty and student health staff at the Robert Wood Johnson Medical School; his mother was a retired high-school guidance counselor. The youngest of four, he had two older sisters, a social worker and an MD, and a brother who had a PhD. If Young hadn't gone to graduate school, he would have been the only one in his family who didn't.

That's not to say he didn't find it "a hump." "It's very serious," he said. "Being a graduate student is intense. You're not playing anymore. You're dealing with your field, your profession. You're interacting with men and women who are known, who've published, who are doing top-notch research. You're dealing with students from all over the country who are serious about the profession. You're more accountable. I have to know what I'm doing, how to diagnose and provide therapy."

His dissertation—on the families of hyperactive children—would come after his generals. He'd been working as a teaching associate; he critiqued the testing techniques of first- and second-year grad students. He'd also been spending thirteen hours a week with Columbus and Central Ohio Psychiatric Hospital patients. The clinical work was what he loved. "Many times I didn't know what to do," he said, "but you develop your style. Now if I hit a wall I can keep a conversation going. Someone may throw me a loop and I have to manage the loop. Or I can fall back on reflections—'You're feeling pretty angry.'

"In general my experience has been good, though whenever I see a patient, race may always be an issue. I haven't met anyone who was totally against seeing me as a therapist because of my skin color."

Geoffrey Young was a black male doctoral student—one of a rare and diminishing ilk. While almost two thirds of all doctorates awarded in the United States went to men, among blacks the proportions were nearly reversed. American black men received 317 PhDs in 1987, compared to 684 in 1977: a 54 percent drop. (In the same period there was a 29 percent decline in the number of doctorates earned by white American men, whose 1987 total was 12,116.)

In the 1980s Ohio State has been third (after Howard University and the University of Michigan) in the number of PhDs awarded to blacks. Ohio State recruits black graduate students—it recruited Geoffrey Young when he was an undergraduate at the predominantly black Hampton Institute (now Hampton University) in Hampton, Virginia. OSU brought him up for a visit, introduced him to faculty in psychology. Once enrolled, he was one of about eight blacks among fifty-two graduate students in clinical psychology. Black faculty were more scarce—Young could think of only one adjunct. "So few black PhDs are interested in academia," he acknowledged. Still deep in the struggles of graduate school, he was not sure that he himself would be interested in staying on the academic treadmill, though he could expect encouragement to do so. His adviser, Steven Beck, had already started.

Young was glad he'd done his undergraduate work in the supportive environs of a black campus where everyone said hello to everyone else. "I would be a liar if I said I never thought I didn't belong here," he said, of his experience at Ohio State. "It's like a city." He didn't know why fewer black males are in college and graduate school, though he did know that people often expected him to be less than he was. "I've had people say, 'I didn't realize you guys were so articulate,'" he said. "It's easy for ignorant people to infer that the dilemma of the black male is self-imposed—that he lacks cognitive intellectual ability and all that crap. Imagine what it's like for a young black male. I have friends—PhD level—we can still walk into a store and be treated as if, 'This is an *animal* type.' It happened in a store yesterday, or I perceived it to happen, and I was dressed just like I am today, in a warm-up suit and a hat with my fraternity letters.

"My role is to be myself, to be the best I can, a black man.

I don't think my role is to save the nation. Among my peers, I'm not the exception."

Ohio State escaped the spate of well-publicized racial incidents on campuses in 1986–88; they occurred at schools like the University of California at Berkeley, the University of Wisconsin at Madison, even Ohio's Oberlin College, one of the first in the country to enroll black students in the nineteenth century. That is not to say that Ohio State was a hotbed of harmony. Provost Myles Brand reported in dismay that a survey in undergraduate residence halls found that 10 percent of the students thought discrimination and prejudice *should* exist. The university, after all, was part of its society.

Because of Ohio State's size, even small percentages of its enrollment become large numbers. The Columbus campus had *thousands* of black students (2,313) in the fall of 1987, but they were a mere 4.4 percent of all students. (The numbers were down 2 percent from the year before and clearly were below the percentage of blacks in the population, almost 11 percent in Ohio.) It also had 76 native Americans, 1,209 Asian- and 529 Hispanic-Americans, 2,756 foreigners, and 43,577 whites: 82 percent of all students were white.

Nationally, huge increases in the numbers of Hispanic and Asian students pushed minority enrollments up during the eighties. This was true also at Ohio State, where Asian students increased by 310 percent over 1977 and Hispanics, by 150 percent, while blacks were *down 19 percent* in numbers and 1.2 percent in enrollment share.

No one had a final explanation for that decline, but Larry Dent, a senior majoring in criminal justice and editor of *Dimensions,* a black student magazine, had some suggestions. He said blacks were uncomfortable on a predominantly white campus, where they missed African-American music, food and, especially, mentors and role models. "It's a relief to go into a class and there's a black instructor," he said, adding,

"He still may give you a hard time." Dent thought university support for a black cultural center might help.

The statistical profile of the student body showed that about three quarters were undergraduates, with the rest in graduate and professional schools. Just under half of all students were women, up from only 36 percent in 1967. The most dramatic rise in women students was in the professional schools, where their percentage was 5 in 1967, 22 in 1977, and 38 in 1987. Of the 80 percent of all students living off campus, a survey found one out of five married, two thirds employed, and the average age a ripe 24.84.

An overwhelming 85.5 percent of the students in Columbus in 1987–88 were from Ohio, but sheer numbers rescued the campus from provincialism. There were 4,709 American students who were not from Ohio, who in fact represented all fifty states with from six (Vermont) to 588 (New York) individuals. Similarly, the 2,756 foreigners gave Ohio State the sixth-highest foreign-student enrollment in the country. The largest number (443) were from Taiwan; Korea was second with 351. Fifty-three thousand students assured diversity. That was not just a matter of race and geography; it was also economic, cultural, political, religious, and social. By its very nature, diversity should be a source of enrichment, an asset to the university.

OSU's powers-that-be—the administration and trustees—saw diversity as a mandate of the founding doctrine, the Morrill Act. They wanted to keep tuition low—for state residents, $630 per quarter in 1987–88; on-campus room and board ran an additional but relatively modest $1,014—to keep the institution *accessible*. Tuition, room, and board for an academic year was $4,932, while comparable charges elsewhere could run as high as Yale University's $17,020. (Through the decade costs at private colleges were rising faster than the cost of living. Said David Breneman, president of Kalamazoo College, "To some degree in this market, people judge quality by price, and a low price at a private college is not necessarily [seen as] a sign of good management." Like cosmetics, colleges often were valued in proportion to price.)

Among the many rewards of diversity was Yilu Liu, a doctoral student in electrical engineering who compared the Ohio State campus to that of Xian Jiao Tong University in mainland China, where she did her undergraduate work. The Ohio State campus reminded her of the one in China, though this one was bigger. When she showed visitors around, she impressed them with an "endless tour." She found classes in Ohio more relaxed—though sometimes an instructor didn't prepare and the class was a waste of time. She was glad for certain differences: Ohio State professors didn't post students' grades alongside their names and the library didn't close for lunch.

When Yilu Liu first arrived in April 1984, she thought jeans looked uncomfortable: "Everybody suffer a little, it looks to me. It's too tight." Along with a sweatshirt and athletic shoes, she herself now wore jeans, though not tight ones. If anything belied student diversity on the Ohio State campus, it was jeans, which were nearly a uniform in fall and winter. So were bookbags.

Yilu Liu was a member of the Chinese Scholar and Student Society, which included almost all mainland Chinese at Ohio State. "We have seminars about American law and music appreciation and extrasensory perception," she said. "Once we went to Cincinnati to have a Ping-Pong match with a Chinese society at the University of Cincinnati. OSU women won. Cincinnati men won."

The Chinese group was one of 440 registered student organizations in 1987–88. These included academic groups (Turfgrass Management, Psychologists for Social Action, Pre-Optometry Club), ethnics (Turkish Students Association), special interest

(Alcoholics Anonymous Friday Group, Children of Holocaust Survivors), religious (Christian Veterinary Fellowship), sports (OSU Trap and Skeet Club), issue-related (Young Socialist Alliance, Gay and Lesbian Alliance).

"I think," said James Murphy, head of OSU Building Services, "youth are getting more to flag, country, and apple pie." National surveys came out showing that the most popular career goal for college freshmen was business (twenty years before it had been education) and that drug use by college students was declining. Margaret Miller, the staff coordinator for Greek Affairs (Ohio State is third in the country in number of Greek chapters), said student interest in sororities had been increasing continuously—in effect, reviving—since 1975. And Sue Miller, secretary to the Undergraduate Student Union, said that during her seven years on the job, students had become more and more conservative: "You do not see a cause-oriented individual much anymore." Almost everyone had an angle on how the 1980s student was a throwback to the era before the late 1960s and early 1970s. The modern student was conservative, a child of the Reagan Age.

Certainly ROTC—the Reserve Officers' Training Corps—was flourishing anew. "I've been fortunate to be in an era when the military is well liked." So said Thomas Wrobleski, a senior majoring in aviation engineering and a Navy ROTC battalion commander. "I've heard all the stories—in the past when any military incidents happened, boom, that was taken out on ROTC people by all our liberal Oval friends. I heard they were spit on or called warmongers. Now, people really have a lot of respect for what you're doing. When the Granada invasion came people wanted to see if you knew anything about it, if you might go over there."

Then too there was the uniform, which he wore all day every Thursday, when drills started at 3 P.M. "Everywhere you walk," Wrobleski said, "they're looking at you. Freshmen haven't seen a guy in a uniform walking around before. It's a great way to meet girls. Guys ask especially about the aviation aspect. They ask if I've ever flown and when I say, 'Yes,' their eyes get wide."

Dressed in his white spring and summer uniform, Wrobleski was seated at a table in an Ohio Union hallway. His hair was short, but although short hair was conspicuous when he arrived in 1984, it wasn't in 1988. The uniform did set him apart. So did his black briefcase—"A bookbag," he explained, "doesn't look as nice with a uniform."

He said that an ROTC unit is supportive. "We have an old-notes and old-tests file. You get help picking classes—I've recommended Linguistics 201 to at least thirty people as an easy, guaranteed A. The unit is exactly like a fraternity in some ways but we hate being called that. When you're in uniform you act a certain way, but we're all very much individuals; you don't have to be there except on Thursdays or when you have a class. Fraternity guys have to fit the image all the time.

"As a freshman you come a week early and have an ROTC orientation, which is like a mini boot camp to knock some sense into you real quick. You learn about customs and courtesies in the military, how to wear your uniform. To teach you discipline, you learn how to march. It's a big shock, out there in September, really hot, with people yelling in your face. I kind of hated it at first. No one else was going through what I was—walking all the way across campus at five in the morning for inspection of your uniform."

Four autumns later Wrobleski was himself in command for freshman orientation. "We had a guy with hair down to the middle of his shoulders and he was wearing an earring. To see him come back a week later with no hair and really looking sharp is a good picture. It's a good feeling to know you're responsible for that. The guy laughs about that now. He caught a lot of abuse during orientation."

For being in ROTC, Wrobleski got his tuition, books, and a hundred dollars a month, but not his room and board. Like half of his class, he hoped to go into naval aviation, even though it meant a six- rather than four-year commitment. In picking aviation Wrobleski was inspired by a movie about navy flyers, *Top Gun*. He owned the tape and had watched it fifty times.

Wrobleski credited ROTC with helping him cope with college: "You get your act together early so you're not floundering around too much." Everyone realizes that some students come to OSU and their act stays in disarray. That happened to a pale, long-haired freshman who arrived on campus after four years in a Catholic boys' high school, which he found equipped him for deft heckling of fundamentalist preachers haranguing students on the Oval. He lived in a residence hall, waited in line for and then despaired of the dining hall food, and enrolled in business, which he didn't like. He was amazed that the average bedtime was 1:30 A.M.; two or three times a week his dorm was enlivened by parties featuring concoctions like hairy buffalo (rum, vodka, and fruit, he said).

Academically, the freshman was impressed to have a professor who was an authority on Thoreau, but he was disdainful of courses that were too easy, like one he took in anthropology. He said, "The night before the exam you read a twenty-page section of the book that she marks out, and then you go in and take the test and get a B. It's a blow-off course." What most impressed him all year, was a springtime rock concert on campus: "We're big enough to attract Pink Floyd," he said. "This university can do anything."

By spring, he was in a mess. A National Merit Commended Scholar, he was at least passing. But he was on conduct probation and lacked direction. "It's a whole year," he reflected.

"It's like getting taller—you don't notice. Maybe the most surprising thing is it's a lot like I expected it to be. I expected not to study all year. I expected to blow off classes. I expected it to be pretty crazy."

One of the most conspicuous students on campus was Scot Zellman, a six-foot five-inch senior, an art major, and the president of the Undergraduate Student Government. As president he was one of the few students ever to step out of the blue-jeans-and-bookbag world and hobnob with people who were running the institution. Dressed in a dark suit, Zellman reported every month to the Board of Trustees and the Senate; he lunched regularly at the Faculty Club with a vice-provost. He had the accoutrements of status: an office in the Ohio Union, the secretarial services of Sue Miller, and a salary of $6,500. And for a year, *his* opinion was the student point of view.

While Zellman became familiar to the people in charge of the university, he actually lost some recognition among students. That was because he used to be a cartoonist doing six strips a week for *The Lantern,* which gave him the kind of name recognition he needed to get elected. Once he was in office, he found that some students wondered what ever happened to him. "How come your strip runs only once a week?"

In the fall Zellman was excited about USG projects—textbook trades, a nighttime escort service, distributing scarlet-and-gray shakers at a football game. By spring, he seemed more skeptical, less ingenuous. He sat in his office with his long legs up and his feet folded on the desk; he smoked and laughed about how, because of a proposal to combat AIDS by installing condom dispensers in residence halls, he was being inundated with condom literature. More seriously, he was pleased that President Jennings had complimented him for efforts to include more black students in USG activities.

But by and large, he was disappointed. "I've met a lot of leaders from other student governments," he said. "At smaller universities they have enormous budgets and power. Huge universities have small, weak student governments like this one. This university is so big that it takes care of everything. It does programming—social events or concerts. It does crime and rape prevention programs. AIDS education. The newspaper is independent. It's a real struggle for the USG to come up with something to do. We're a storage house, a warehouse for bodies to serve on university-wide committees. 'Scot, we need an undergraduate over here.' You begin to feel like a dispatcher."

Like everyone else, Scot Zellman called these conservative times on campus, though he thought "the conservative wave is starting to ebb—Students for Peace and Justice is more active now." Because of diversity, even in a conservative era Ohio State had Students for Peace and Justice, though the leader, Kim Fullman, liked to think that "people are waking up."

A senior majoring in political science, Kim Fullman wore two tiny silver earrings—a peace symbol on the left, a female symbol on the right. Sitting at a table in the King Avenue Coffee Shop, an eclectic, appropriately modest vegetarian restaurant just off campus, she ordered a cup of tea and recalled how she transferred from her hometown University of Cincinnati in winter 1986, in the hope of finding "some great groups out of the political mainstream." When she did find Students for Peace and Disarmament (as it was then known), it was a discussion group in a "low-energy period." The first time she went, of the six people attending, three were high-school students from Worthington studying radicalism. Now, two years later, the group had grown to about thirty active members. Fullman said that, being nonhierarchical, it couldn't grow too much without veering into chaos.

Students for Peace and Justice tried to expand peace awareness with marches to commemorate Hiroshima, with the world's largest human peace sign on the Oval, with protests against war taxes and CIA recruiters on campus. Ultimately they met twice with President Jennings, which led to university funding for a covert-action forum that they cosponsored spring quarter 1988. "We raised the consciousness of a lot of people," Fullman said of that event. "It's the apathetic student that's our worst enemy. We have to show these people there's more to life than BMWs."

She concluded that the forum was more effective than a protest: "When you just demonstrate, you get into left-wing rhetoric and people aren't listening. And a lot of students see demonstrations and think, 'Oh, God, that's risky.' Or they say, 'Well, where do they think they're getting off? Do they think this is the *sixties?'*

"Our fundraiser was called Time Machine to the Sixties. Three hundred people came—about two hundred more than we usually have—and after expenses we made four hundred dollars. There was a lot of discussion about the theme because we already have this throwback image. But we decided to do it because there's a lot of sixties nostalgia—you see students wearing peace signs and tie-dye.

"The fundraiser had bands, a best-sixties costume prize, a trivia contest, and we showed some videos—'Battleground OSU,' a documentary about the 1970 student demonstrations. It shows our campus—all the buildings you recognize, the Oval, Neil Avenue—and students—thousands of students are standing around yelling. And you see the National Guard with their rifles drawn. You see students being arrested and dragged away. There was a lot of violence. We wanted to show that to the people who say, 'Oh, the sixties. It was so nice.'"

In May Kim Fullman became one of the President's Undergraduate Leadership Award Recipients when she was cited as a woman Student Organization Officer. She said later that she was surprised. There were eighty nominees, and she was out of the mainstream.

In August and September, Geoffrey Young took and passed his generals, his doctoral exams. The written series began the morning of Wednesday, August 31, when he chose two out of three questions and then wrote for three hours on psychopathology. That afternoon, it was psychological assessment; the next day, psychological intervention and research methodology. He finished Friday with ethics and minority issues. Altogether, he spent fifteen hours writing and later, when he typed out his answers, they came to forty-five pages.

His orals, a defense of these written answers, came three weeks later, when five professors, including his adviser, questioned him for two hours one morning. "There's such a large amount of material in my head now," Young said afterward. "But when you relearn it all, it's more relevant, it makes sense. I hated the process, the pressure. But in retrospect, it was good: I could do it."

Was he nervous for the orals? He said he was surprised that he felt fairly confident. But after all, he pointed out, with all that reading in psychotherapy, it was just a matter of self help.

JANUARY CALENDAR

Cold Snap. Winter quarter classes began Monday, January 4, and the weather turned cold; by Wednesday the forecast was for a high of 16 and a low of 0. McCracken Power Plant was pumping steam to heat all the buildings on central and ag campuses; output reached 322,000 pounds an hour the first week of January. That turned out to be the season's peak, though it was below 1983's all-time record. A picture of Andrew Hanes, a freshman from Pittsburgh, ice skating on the Olentangy River made the front page of *The Lantern* on Friday. In the next issue, Monday's, the paper ran a thin-ice warning from safety officials, though on page 13.

Goodbye, Columbus. The weather may or may not have influenced a poll the paper ran that month. When the inquiring photographer went out and asked three seniors, a junior, a graduate student, and a freshman if they would like to stay in Columbus after graduation, only the freshman said yes.

Global Jiggles. "The Greenwich Meridian today is still near the old Greenwich Observatory Building," said Ivan Mueller, professor and geodesist. "But it's not marked because it's constantly moving. It's a moving reference line. That's the whole problem—that nothing on this earth is fixed." So Mueller had helped found the International Earth Rotation Service (IERS). As of January 1, IERS was determining the exact location of the Greenwich Meridian—0 degrees longitude—by extraterrestrial means, such as radio signals from remote stars or quasars. The new monitoring would be accurate enough to account for earthly jiggles: the wobble in the axis and the kind of surface fluctuation that moved Greenwich 2.5 centimeters farther away from South America every year.

This Space Is Mine. Parking became hazardous in January: Arguments over spaces led to two cases of assault and one of threatening with a baseball bat.

In the Basket. On January 7, the men's basketball team lost its Big Ten opener, an away game against Purdue, even though junior Jay Burson scored twenty-four points and senior Curtis Wilson, twenty. The women's basketball team did better the next night; it won its home game against Indiana, 83–70. Jay Burson was named Big Ten Player of the Week on January 19. Of Burson, who at six feet, 158 pounds, was small for a basketball player, Coach Gary Williams said, "I'd rather have those guys that look a little funny out there, but the ball winds up in the basket."

Board Students? Down at the Statehouse, the Ohio Senate Education Committee began hearings on having two nonvoting student trustees on state university boards. For sixteen years the bill had been blocked in the committee, which now had a new chairman. Although thirty-six states and the District of Columbia already had student trustees, OSU Trustee Hamilton J. Teaford said he was against it. He assumed the Ohio bill wouldn't pass this time either.

Lost Before the Kickoff. The new football coach, John Cooper, arrived in January for the hectic final weeks of recruiting and found himself lost. "We were having the visiting kids stay at the Hyatt on Capitol Square, and I didn't even know how to get there," he said later.

Martin Luther King Day. The OSU Peace Network sent a

busful of thirty-five students and faculty to join the Columbus Martin Luther King Day march January 18, and President Jennings got a distinguished service award from the Black Clergy of Greater Cleveland for the university's affirmative action program. Said Jennings, "We can best realize Dr. King's dream by acknowledging that diversity is necessary to the creation of educated men and women."

Rush to the Bar. In what appeared to be a nationwide trend, law-school applications were up 37 percent. Law Dean Francis Beytagh said he thought there was more behind the increases than "L.A. Law."

Historical Footnote. At the end of the month, Jennings addressed the University Senate. "In the days since mid-November," he said, "I have seen the university community live through a broken moment, repair itself, and come back together. What we passed through in November and December is but a sentence, even a phrase, in the long historical narrative of this university." Afterward, in an expression of, at least, hope, his audience gave him a standing ovation.

CHAPTER 5

Money and the Pursuit of Knowledge

The scope of research is limited only by imagination and tools of perception. Take Ohio State's radio telescope—nicknamed the Big Ear—which is about twenty miles north of campus in Delaware County. It's half a mile back from the road; you don't see it until after you've passed through a small, dark woods of pine trees. Then suddenly, improbably, it looms on the far side of a field. Its two reflectors look like drive-in movie screens with an empty parking lot between them.

Once you've crossed the field for a closer look, you find that the big rectangular screens are really a wire mesh like that in cot springs. Framed and supported by steel pipes and girders, they're eight stories high and almost three hundred feet long. The flat surface between them, some two football fields in area, is level, paved, covered with aluminum, and encroached upon by half a dozen two-foot weeds. When the wind blows, the big screens vibrate and you can hear them whine. The sound is eerie—almost other worldly.

But then, the Big Ear is on an other-worldly mission. In a quest perhaps preposterous and certainly ambitious, it's listening for intelligent signals from another planet; what it hopes to find are other civilizations. It's been doing this since 1973 and Robert Dixon, an OSU staffer who has been with the project from the beginning, says that it hasn't yet found anything for sure. "If we had," he says, "everyone on earth would know about it."

Research is a quest for new knowledge—which may be newly reknowing. Take A. E. Wallace Maurer, an OSU English professor who's been helping to edit the University of California edition of the works of John Dryden, the seventeenth-century English poet, dramatist, and essayist. To explain everything a modern reader wouldn't understand, Maurer has spent years researching seventeenth-century England. "The principle," he says, "has been to do all that's mortally possible to get to the bottom of things."

Research goes to the past, the present, and the future, to the physical and metaphysical. Take yellow nutsedge. Leo Bendixen, a professor of agronomy, has spent a quarter century getting to the bottom of a weed called yellow nutsedge, which reproduces underground and does so so successfully that it is the fifth worst weed in the United States and sixteenth worst in the world. As Maurer became intimate with the seventeenth century, Bendixen became intimate with yellow nutsedge. The radio telescope's Dixon acknowledges that he is not yet intimate with extraterrestrial life, even though a university directory of people who know things lists him as an expert. Extraterrestrial life, he says, "is a science that has yet to get its first data point." He's working on it.

Research goes everywhere. Everywhere, that is, that money will let it go. What makes Ohio State research happen is money—in sometimes huge but often relatively small amounts, such as Wallace Maurer's living expenses when he had to go to California.

When Scot Zellman, president of the Undergraduate Student Government, started going to meetings of the Board of Trustees, he found that money and research—two spheres remote from his undergraduate constituency—were the university's prime concerns. "I wondered about the priority list," he said. "Which comes first, research or students? Or both? I get aggravated when I hear about money being poured into research grants and some aspect of student life is suffering, like the libraries or the renovation of classrooms."

In discerning a potential conflict between research and teaching, Zellman had come upon one of the ongoing dilemmas in higher education: Can research and teaching live together? Or does a university have to pick one over the other? No less than the reputation of the institution is at stake—its ability to attract the best students and more money, even the value of its degrees. "Among the first two tiers of universities," says OSU sociologist Ronald Corwin, "the real currency is prestige. They get that through research."

Corwin says that he believes that research and teaching are compatible: "Universities are here to create knowledge as well as to train students; conveying information is not in conflict with research. I would be uncomfortable with faculty that never writes—you don't know what they're thinking. The problem is that you get this tension between teaching and research. The tension is in motivating students who aren't sure they're interested—that goes along with mass education. In large universities like this you have a lot of students who aren't sure they want to be there."

At Ohio State, all faculty are supposed to be judged—and specifically, to get tenure—on the basis of teaching, service, and research. John Davis, the classics professor who teaches large and small classes, said research counts most: "Essentially, if you can teach decently and the chairman isn't getting nasty letters on you, then teaching is pass-fail. Committee work is the second phase; it's called service. There are a million committees here. That's pass-fail. Then we get down to research. That's where the real evaluation is." Davis was in the process of publishing a monograph arguing that the poems of Ovid's *Amores* were written to be read aloud. "I'm tenured so I can take my good old time," he said. "But it's increasingly important for new faculty to publish, so in classics a lot of half-baked stuff is getting ground out. This is a well-plowed field."

Measured in dollars, research is big business at Ohio State. In 1987–88, the university was developing a $37.5 million supercomputer center and building a $54 million cancer research hospital slated to be the country's fourth largest. And it was spending a total of $125.5 million on research. (Incidentally, the same year Columbus campus student fees were more: $133.3 million.) Most research money was in the $99 million Research Foundation budget, which was up 73 percent in the decade and more than five times 1970's $17.5 million.

Other universities were also seeing a surge in research spending, and one reason was money from state and federal governments. In Ohio, for instance, in the spring of 1988, the General Assembly approved $22 million for a next-generation machine for the Ohio Supercomputer Center on the OSU campus; that was on top of $15.7 million the state and university had already spent on supercomputing.

William Coulter, chancellor of the Board of Regents—a state agency which links Ohio colleges and state government—had an explanation for Ohio's munificence: "In the last four to five years, there's been a dawning, a perception that higher education is a part of the solution to our problems of economic resurgence, rather than the source of them. People believe universities produce basic research. Technologies flow from it and are the basis for economic development." The dawning came to the governor, the leaders of both parties, the public. It was hardly exclusive to Ohio, Coulter said, but it had a big impact there because of the acute Rust-Belt syndrome in the early 1980s. "We had a tremendous loss in basic industries on which the state rested for decades when people were able to maintain their families with good jobs and without a lot of education."

The federal government was also something of a research sugar daddy in the 1980s, especially through agencies like the National Science Foundation. "Nowadays," said Ivan Mueller of Geodetic Science and Surveying, "the name of the game is large grants as opposed to the smaller grants that used to be typical. These large centers have a better chance of getting funding." Mueller knew what he was talking about. In 1986 he'd brought Ohio State a Center for the Commercial Development of Space, launched with a five-million-dollar five-year nest egg from NASA for real-time mapping research. Interdisciplinary centers with industry, government, and university funding—like this one—were a White House idea. That didn't hurt.

To get the NASA grant, Mueller first had to be assured of state support, so he started running down to the Statehouse and buttonholing politicians. He got a letter from the governor promising $100,000 if the NASA money came through. After OSU submitted its proposal to NASA, Mueller and his cohorts set upon Congressmen: Senators Howard Metzenbaum and John Glenn; Representatives John Kasich, Chalmers Wylie, Louis Stokes. "We went to Republican, Democrat, everybody in sight. I wrote letters. I talked myself to Wylie and Kasich and Metzenbaum. A dean called Glenn. We always tried to find somebody who knew somebody." In the end, everyone they approached called NASA. Mueller is sure that all twenty-five proposals that NASA got had political support, but only five were selected; of those, he later heard, OSU was first on the list.

But of course, money is just a beginning, a token of intent; the real key to research is in *minds*—largely, in hiring faculty. Sociologist Corwin talks about the hiring game that can result. "My department will try to get someone in demography, say," he says. "We'll look for someone with prestige, who can attract resources. They publish, which brings visibility, and then we can go out and hire other people. We can compete with Stanford and Chicago if a student wants to be a demographer." Corwin believes that lately the Sociology Department—having competed successfully with other departments for resources, as he would say—has done some good hiring. In just four years, he says, four new people have taken the department from nowhere to the top in economic sociology.

For the researcher, research often is more obsession than work—at any career stage. "There is nothing I'd rather do," says Melvin Newman. "Whatever you find out is new." Newman is a chemist who comes in every day and, dressed in a white lab coat and navy blue tennis shoes, works with organic compounds. That would be less remarkable if Newman hadn't had to retire at seventy ten years ago. "Most people that I've observed, are very lonely for a while when they retire," Newman says. "I've never had that problem."

During his career, Newman has published 350 papers and directed the theses of 110 PhDs. Now the university provides his chemicals, his office, and the lab across the hall that he shares with a postdoctoral fellow. His bench there holds a dizzy array of brown bottles, flasks, synthetic rubber stoppers, glass tubes. A brown liquid is being heated; a yellow one is in ice water.

What Newman wants to do is synthesize a hydrocarbon with forty-one characters in its name and a structure that he admires. He is applying for an NSF grant but he says an emeritus doesn't have a preferred spot. In any case, he will keep pursuing the hydrocarbon. "It's the toughest job I've ever been associated with," he says. "Getting the grant would make it quicker." Which, when you're eighty, is a consideration.

Melvin Newman marked a full half century at OSU in autumn 1986, the year that Robert E. Page, Jr. arrived. An assistant professor of entomology, Page runs the Bee Laboratory. He can't get enough of his work. He finds it hard to relax in front of a television; he works evenings and weekends. Why? The first reason is "corny," he says. "It's the thrill of discovery. The basic curiosity behind what I do." He calls "ego" his second motive: "the peer acceptance, going to meetings where people have read my papers and I'm invited to give talks." And finally, there's "insecurity—not knowing when enough is enough. As if more papers are more success." Insecurity may come partly from not having tenure, even though he has published a lot—fifty papers in just eight years.

Page oversees one of eight U.S. research groups in bee behavior. "I'm in a field that's very competitive," he says. "I have to make my decisions on what's the cutting edge and let's get this out fast before someone beats us to it." Bee behaviorists today are overturning the traditional concept of the hive as a harmonious superorganism, with each insect meaningful only as a component of the whole. The latest research finds hives rife with nepotism and family ties: Page has found that in rearing prospective queens, bees take better care of their full sisters than of their half sisters.

When Leo Bendixen first started studying the weed yellow nutsedge in 1962, he chose it partly because at that time, no one else in the United States was working on it. By 1987, he was no longer alone, but he was necessarily senior. Asked what yellow nutsedge looked like, he jumped up from his desk and moved at great speed down the hall to a window. "See that lighter grass there along the sidewalk? Yes? Now I've sensitized you. You'll see it everywhere." He was right. Yellow nutsedge looks more or less like grass, except that it is lighter in color—a yellowish green—and in turf, because it grows faster, it is a little taller than the other grass.

Yellow nutsedge sends out six or eight underground rhizomes—slender strands that grow outward behind pointed ends and then rise to the surface and form new plants. The new plants in turn are sending out rhizomes within three weeks; within five weeks they are parents. The pointed rhizomes are sharp enough to pierce a potato or a carrot or a peanut, spoil its looks, sicken it, and give yellow nutsedge a bad name.

Bendixen has been most entranced by the peppercorn-sized tubers that develop toward autumn at the rhizome ends. The tubers contain eight buds that will winter over, waiting for spring, when they take turns sprouting. Because more always seem to be waiting to sprout, these tubers account for yellow nutsedge's success. Once Bendixen saw yellow nutsedge growing on a lawn in his neighborhood—the weed occupied a ten-by-twelve-foot patch in the middle of the yard. The property owner's lawn service applied a herbicide that also killed the grass, so the lawn service came back to reseed. But the lawn service apparently didn't know about the tubers that lurk in the soil. When the grass grew back, so did the nutsedge.

Bendixen's office is in Kottman Hall on west campus, three quarters of a mile due west of Denney Hall, where Wallace Maurer has a fifth-floor office. There Maurer keeps not only the usual bookcases and desk, but also his three-speed 1971 bicycle and two brown boxes, one of which holds a computer he doesn't use (the screen is out but not connected) and the other of which contains six hundred pages of notes (handwritten) for a book he would like to write on John Dryden's long poem, *Absalom and Achitophel*. It is June, so the professor's kelly-green slacks are seasonal, but he rides the bicycle year-round.

Maurer arrived at Ohio State thirty-five years ago, in 1953, a lowly assistant instructor with a still not quite finished University of Wisconsin dissertation on John Dryden's view of history, which he culled from the late nineteenth-century, eighteen-volume Scott-Saintsbury edition of Dryden's works. A new twenty-volume edition is now being prepared at the University of California at Los Angeles. It was begun in the late 1940s by two professors who have since died and been succeeded by General Editor Alan Roper; and although the first volume published came out in 1956, four remain to be done. Maurer was a coeditor for one volume; he is editor of another, which contains six prose works from the 1690s. When Maurer finished working on it in 1987 (publication was to take another two years), Ohio State commended him with a raise.

"I think," Maurer says, "that this is the most meticulous and painstaking single-author edition of the twentieth century." For example, Dryden mentioned oranges, so Maurer came up with a long footnote on the seventeenth-century orange trade. In the course of his researches, Maurer got microfilms from England and made four trips to California and libraries there; but from 1978 on, his Dryden Headquarters was a table in the Main Library's Rare Books Room. He came in every day, for an hour or two when he was teaching, 8 A.M. to 5 P.M. during summer quarter; and nine years passed before he quit the table. "One time I figured for every solid line I've written, I've walked a quarter mile through the stacks collecting information," he says. To edit one volume, he consulted eleven hundred works.

"There are," Maurer says, "half a dozen of us on this side of the Atlantic who if put in a room would have the stuff on Dryden." He has never been to England, though; this man who braves the twelve-mile trips from his home on a bicycle is nervous of flying. Even so, he knows Dryden ("One of the people I know best"), his times ("The era has to be reconstructed"), his contemporaries (like one Richard Mulys, who "could never have suspected that three hundred years later someone would come along and rummage in his private life").

Wallace Maurer does have some advantage over Robert Dixon and the Big Ear, in that at least he is rummaging in a known civilization; finding unknown ones is trickier. The first problem is that, before the Big Ear can find other civilizations, it must find its wherewithal in this one. It is not enough to delight the imagination, though that does help provide a cadre of twenty volunteers from on and off campus. (Some were recruited by a flyer that read, VOLUNTEERS NEEDED!!! SEARCH FOR EXTRA-TERRESTRIAL INTELLIGENCE/THIS IS NOT A JOKE!) Even Robert Dixon, who has a doctorate in electrical engineering and in his earthly life is deputy director of the Instruction and Research Computer Center—that's academic computing services—is a volunteer. Every week he spends ten to fifteen hours of lunch, after-work and weekend time on the radio telescope, whose programming he masterminds.

Ohio State helps by paying the telescope's electric bill and providing office and storage space on campus. A fifteen-thousand-dollar annual grant comes from NASA; with donations, it goes for maintenance and secretarial help. Some money comes from mail-order sales of astronomical reference material; for a while, they tried to make money with a magazine— *Cosmic Search*—but it went broke.

The Big Ear was built in the early 1960s by OSU Radio Astronomer John Kraus, now an emeritus professor. For most of a decade it worked on the Ohio Sky Search, which scanned the entire sky for sources of natural radiation and mapped the twenty-thousand it found. (One, OH 471, for a while held the record as the most distant known object in the universe.) Then in 1973, Kraus and Dixon launched the Big Ear on the earth's only full-time search for extraterrestrial life. In the mid-1980s it was joined by a Harvard University radio telescope, which Dixon says is smaller but has better computers. How the two telescopes search reflects their sponsoring institutions: Ohio State covers a large frequency range; Harvard a narrower one, though with greater sensitivity.

Big Ear's two large reflectors are not the same. The screen to the north is flat and can be tilted up and down; that's how it's aimed. The second reflector, which is stationary, is curved in the shape of a parabola to focus the radio waves onto feed horns on the flat aluminum-covered surface. The feed horns relay the signals to receivers and computers in an underground room. For years the computers there spewed out printouts that showed fifty columns (for fifty channels) of tiny, scratchy numbers and letters: 1 to 9, then A to Z as a signal got stronger. Weak signals—1, 2, or 3—were just random noise; above 4 was "more interesting," Dixon says.

Once, in August 1977, there was a signal—6 E Q U J 5—that went way above "interesting" to the "WOW!" that volunteer Jerry Ehman wrote on the printout margin when he saw it a few days later. "We all got very excited," Dixon says. "It had all the hallmarks of a signal from another civilization except one—it was never there again. We went back and looked hundreds of times and never saw anything. It was not a hoax, a fluke, an equipment malfunction. But it could have been man-made—some super-secret satellite in solar orbit. We do know secret things go on.

"A single large number, or strong signal, is a 'bump.' We have found a lot of those. We made a map of them. If random, they should appear uniformly across the entire sky. But they show a definite relation to our galaxy—we see more if we look at the galactic poles. I don't think this has anything to do with other civilizations, but you know in science important discoveries are often made by accident. This may be a new phenomenon—a property of our galaxy that no one knew about before. Or it could be a fluke.

"I'd like to repeat that experiment. It's our intention to do that. Thus we've changed the way we do things." In 1987–88 the radio telescope was getting a new, though second-hand, computer—a donation—and programming it to listen better to unusual signals. Furthermore, it would tune in not just fifty but three thousand channels and have the capacity to zoom in on a frequency; and it wouldn't continue to print out everything. "Though I'm not sure we'll find them, I really believe there are other civilizations out there," Dixon says. But knowing the best way to look is "a difficult problem. We're gaining experience. Man is just beginning."

Dixon observes that "this is a subject of great interest to the average person." Once a month he gets a call from a reporter somewhere; all the major television networks have visited. The BBC came once too; Dixon says they made a special effort: "They created a model of the galaxy with Cadillac convertibles driving around in the field next to the telescope. They had me in the back of one. I had a loudspeaker on a wire that I swung around my head. I was the sun and the loudspeaker was the earth. The narrator was in another Cadillac swinging his microphone around—he was another star and his microphone was another planet and we were both driving around the center of the galaxy.

"One Cadillac got stuck in the mud, and a tow truck came and got stuck. The observatory crane pulled them both out."

FEBRUARY CALENDAR

Tracey Hall's Smile. The instant before Tracey Hall broke the all-time career scoring record in women's basketball, *Lantern* photographer John Canady took her picture. It shows her midair, her arm outstretched, the ball just above her fingers. In the background the spectators' faces are somber, watching intently. Only Hall is grinning; she was the only one who already *knew* the ball would go in. After it did, the February 14 game against Michigan was stopped, and the previous record holder, Kim Jordan, who played from 1976–80 and was now head coach at Cornell, gave the game ball to Hall.

At the end of the season, Hall's scoring record stood at 1,912 points. By then attendance for women's basketball had also set a record: 69,727 people watched fifteen home games. The total for sixteen men's games was 209,286.

Meals, Old Wars, and Snow. During the first week of February, Ohio State dining halls served 100,504 meals. Altogether, 3.2 million breakfasts, lunches, and dinners were dished out in 1987–88.

A history symposium February 5 took a new look at "Ancient Society and War." Participants reassessed the Persian Wars in Greece and the military defeat of Republican Rome.

And after a two-inch snowstorm on the eleventh, crews

worked all night to put three tons of salt on campus sidewalks and forty-eight tons on roads. Chuck Smith, grounds maintenance superintendent, complained, "The hardest part is that this place never sleeps, and there are always people on the road."

Skull Beggary. Human skulls were in short supply, so the dental school, which used them in class, tried advertising in its alumni *Quarterly*. "Any type skull will do," the ad said, "although we would prefer those with all their parts, 32 teeth, etc." However, alumni hung onto their skulls (which years ago were easy to get). Only eight came in—far fewer than the fifty hoped for. The eight were mostly from elderly dentists no longer in practice. They all got credit for a $165 contribution.

Grade-A Bobsled. A bobsled that started out as a class project in Industrial Design 462.04 (Product Design) went to the Winter Olympics in Calgary, though not before the original scarlet and gray paint was covered over with blue, the U.S. team's official color. Said to be the favorite of Brent Rushlaw, the top American driver, the OSU sled did well in ten preliminary runs before it was disqualified. A judge thought it might damage the track because of unusual bumpers. Anyway, everyone in that design class got an A.

Current Events. Rick Bay, who resigned as athletic director to protest the firing of Earle Bruce, took an administrative job with the New York Yankees in mid-February.

Students living in dormitories were complaining about the new telephones: Incoming calls were cut off. A spokesman for Telephone Services said that the phones were all right; callers must be hanging up.

Mummy on the Oval. "Ever since I first came here," said Jon Hill, a senior and art student, "the Oval has intrigued me. It's just a bunch of anonymous people walking back and forth—the accentuation of loneliness that one can get at this campus." Thus on the afternoon of Tuesday, the twenty-third, Hill, wrapped completely in tape so that he looked like a mummy, lay down on his back in the middle of the Oval. He was offering a performance art work entitled *Isolation and Loneliness.* Passersby who stopped to console him removed pieces of tape.

Two for a Day. On the twenty-fourth, Robert Leugers, also a senior, was President for a Day, which meant that he spent the day with President Jennings. After sitting in on a meeting between Jennings and a member of the Columbus Urban League, Leugers said he hadn't expected Jennings "to be so open about his job." Jennings said he used the annual occasion to get the student's appraisal of OSU.

412 Beginnings. The first orientation program for students planning to enroll in the spring was February 26. By the time spring quarter began, four sessions had accommodated more transfers (223) than freshmen (189).

Can Spring Be Far Behind? On Saturday, the twenty-seventh, spring was in the offing: The baseball team went to Louisville for its first game of the season.

CHAPTER 6

Renaissance Buckeye

One of Charles Csuri's favorite photos of himself shows him seated in the corner of a room. The setting is spare and ambiguous—for instance, a black rectangle at the right disappears out of the picture before it's recognizable. He's sitting with his arms and legs crossed, so that he looks reserved, which he is; his legs, stretched out toward the camera, look long so that he looks tall, which he is. He's wearing business clothes—a suit without the coat, the shirt sleeves rolled up. He looks up at the photographer; his expression is serious, perhaps annoyed. The picture has no obvious clues at all, as to who he is. Perhaps that's why he likes it. It doesn't limit him.

Certainly, he has an unusual background. He is an artist trained both in art and technology: He bridges art and science. Because he does, Ohio State is a leader in computer graphics research; it has helped invent computer graphics. This would not be so if it weren't for football. In 1940 Ohio State recruited Charles Csuri to play football; because of football, he went to college and became an artist. Football is the mother of computer graphics. Well, at least partly.

Csuri arrived at Ohio State in 1940. Except for three years during World War II, he has been at the university ever since—by the summer of 1988, that's forty-eight years. He has done almost everything there is to do at Ohio State. He has studied, taught, researched, and administered. He has used the freedom of tenure to go radical. He has hobnobbed creatively with a colleague in a different discipline. He found his wife. And of course, he played football. In fact, he was All-American.

Now he is laden with titles. He is a professor in two departments—art education and computer science—and he heads the Advanced Computing Center for the Arts and Design (ACCAD). Ohio State has honored him. It gave him its Distinguished Research Award; it asked him to speak at a commencement. For his part, although he has been asked to work for other institutions, Csuri has chosen not to leave Ohio State, not even to retire, which, for someone born in 1922, might have been an option. He says, "What I'm doing is just beginning."

In 1988, after twenty years of directing computer graphics research, Csuri could look around and see the research center he wrought in place—fourteen thousand square feet under the mauve girders and ginger-colored duct pipes of a brand-new building. So, for the first time since 1969, he began to work again as an artist. He was attracted to computer graphics in the first place because of its artistic potential, but in 1964 its potential was limited by the very newness of the field. Now research had opened once unimagined artistic possibilities which no one else seemed to be taking advantage of. He could do something utterly unique, something original and witty. He had before.

Computer graphics is telling a computer to make pictures. It is, Csuri says, "converting the numeric into a geometric representation." For an architect, computer graphics can picture a building; for a chemist, a molecule; for an engineer, wind resistance. Computer graphics has been used to make flight simulators that train pilots, to educate the deaf, to produce special effects for television and movies. Just as it may have huge potential in fields such as science, education, and entertainment (after all, the next Mickey Mouse may be a matter of data), it also has enormous possibilities for an artist. With a computer, the artist can manipulate light, lines, color—in fact, everything.

Csuri first did computer art in the late sixties, when, over a five-year period, he produced a remarkable—and necessarily innovative—body of work. Specifically, he made line drawings to explore the particular character of the computer—its capacity for tireless repetition, for chance placement, for altering lines. *Flypaper* represented 825 flies scattered randomly across the page. It was deliberately dumb, machinelike, and ridiculous—"I would never make a *painting* of 825 flies." In another study of chance—*Random War*—the message was serious. The toy soldiers, half of them black, half red, got their assignments from a random number generator. They remained standing; or, tilted at a 45-degree angle, they were wounded; or, lying down, they were dead.

Csuri also explored transformations. He would assign equal line segments to two drawings of the same size—an angel and a devil. Then the computer could transform the devil into the angel, or vice-versa. Or it could take an explosion of dots and squiggles and show five stages of resolving them into a hummingbird. It could show nine steps of aging, from a young woman's face to an old woman's. It could distort a figure's legs until they were very short or very long. Necessarily innovative at the time, these pictures seem fresh and insightful even twenty years later. Even before the computer, Csuri had had a respectable career as an artist—for the ten years before 1965 he showed art with moderate success in New York—but it is fitting that the one work of his that the Museum of Modern Art has is a computer graphics film from the sixties, "Hummingbird."

Csuri's computer art from the sixties does show how primitive computer graphics was at the time. He had to use wire-like line drawings, because that's what he *could* use. He could have added some rudimentary shading. But certainly at that time nothing moved, color was dictated by the pen in the plotter and everything was two-dimensional.

In the seventies people began using data to "sculpt" three-dimensional objects in the computer—a cube, say, that could be seen from all angles. By the eighties screens were showing animation: a skeleton doing a broad jump. Thanks to "flexible-body dynamics" flags rippled in the wind or soap bubbles bounced on the floor; "rigid-body dynamics" could make chairs fall down stairs. Images could be mapped onto objects; objects could be seen from all sides; it all happened in color; it all evolved at OSU. Charles Csuri made it possible.

That is not to say the job is finished, for the technology is still evolving. Csuri jumps up from his desk and lopes out to the hall, around a corner, and into a small, darkened room where he flips a switch and illumines a computer screen. A picture appears: colored lights, an aquarium, two fish swimming back and forth. "This is where we are—this is state of the art, a real-time event," he says. But he's laughing, for the aquarium not only looks real, it is real: at once a joke and a goal.

A nun in New York is writing her PhD dissertation on Charles Csuri. She is Sister Jean Dominici DeMaria; her dissertation is for New York University. DeMaria, who herself teaches art at Molloy College, admires Csuri as a teacher ("He doesn't keep his knowledge of computer graphics to himself"). Herself a researcher, she admires the way he raised money ("He has such a history in grant development"). She defends Csuri for using technology—the computer—in art. He wasn't the first artist to use technology; Leonardo worked with math and perspective. "One of the points I'm going to make," DeMaria says, "is that Csuri is like a Renaissance Man."

For an artist, Csuri has a lot of background in technology. It began with high school. Growing up in a Hungarian immigrant family, Csuri thought he would be a machinist ("That's what all the kids did") so he went to Cleveland's West Technical High School and studied shop math and pattern making. During World War II he had more technical training. Before the Army decided it had to have him in the infantry on the European front, the Air Corps sent him to Newark College of Engineering (now the New Jersey Institute of Technology). In a year he did two years' engineering. He studied chemistry, physics, and lots of math—college algebra, trigonometry, analytical geometry, differential calculus; he thinks he was not far from a degree.

Csuri was an artist first, though. As a boy who loved drawing, he spent Saturday mornings on Cleveland street cars going to museum classes; certainly from the time he first walked into a studio at Ohio State, he was an artist. He majored in art at OSU and got a master's degree in it after the war. Though he has advised doctoral students, the master's is a terminal degree in studio art and he never did get a doctorate. People often mistakenly call him "Doctor." "Professor is correct," he says. "Chuck is fine."

Csuri began to teach drawing and painting at Ohio State in 1947. In one of his painting classes he found a wife, a woman from Alabama named Shirley Echols, whom he calls Lee. (She is also an artist, represented by a carved wooden sculpture and two paintings in her husband's office.) Csuri believes that when he got tenure in the mid-fifties, it was for his teaching; by 1963 he was a full professor.

Certainly, he took teaching seriously. He tried to teach spontaneity by giving his students one-inch charcoals to draw bold and simple lines. Or by having them pull instructions out of a bag or throw darts to decide where squares of color would go. He dispensed advice: "You're better off if you have a general idea of the end product, rather than a specific one." "The moment you have trouble is when you think 'Gee, this is really good.' Then you become protective and conservative psychologically. You're dead."

For an artist with Csuri's background in technology, it was perfectly natural to use the computer to make art. Even beforehand, in the late fifties and early sixties, he was experimenting with machines. For instance, he tried pantographs— pairs of mechanically controlled pens. Thomas Jefferson used a pantograph to make simultaneous copies of his letters. Csuri adapted it so that as one pen drew a true figure, the other etched a distorted version.

But while using machines may have been natural for Csuri, it seemed unnatural to the art department. From their point of view, a machine inevitably took the art out of art. They thought that to use machines meant "dehumanization," Csuri says. "It was boring. It was cold. There was no emotion. You couldn't possibly have emotion when you didn't have control as you did with a brush.

"I was fortunate that I was a full professor with tenure. I didn't have to worry about their perception of my productivity. I just went ahead. I didn't question my basic ability as an artist. I was one of the few faculty members who had New York shows and got at least moderate critical acclaim." In the early seventies he changed departments and switched from Art to Art Education. Since 1986 computer graphics has been an independent unit, the ACCAD.

Sister Jean Dominici DeMaria reports that she also confronted an art-science tension when she first proposed Csuri as her dissertation subject. Her advisers were concerned because "they didn't consider him a fine artist. The National Endowment for the Arts wouldn't even look at anybody using machinery." The climate at NYU changed, she says, when two administrators from Ohio State came to work there. They brought with them OSU's institutional faith in computer graphics.

Ohio State doesn't recruit football players to cultivate research professors. That would be crazy; it doesn't happen. Though it did once.

Csuri was recruited in style. He was brought to Columbus and introduced not only to the president of the university but also to the governor. It was dazzling. Before he knew it, he was signed up for classes. Ohio State didn't have athletic scholarships in 1940. What it offered were co-op houses, where a dozen students could hire a cook and share the cleaning, and work programs with little work. Such "work" made for a deceptive, guilt-provoking situation that still makes Csuri feel uneasy. He is a circumspect type, so he now thinks of football as sexist, as "something out of the Christians and the lions." But for the son of an immigrant shoemaker, football was the key to an education.

In the fall of 1942, six months before he was drafted, Csuri was a junior and a first-string tackle for OSU's first national champion football team. He made All American that year, though he values more being voted Most Valuable Player by his teammates. He recalls a Father's Day game against Pittsburgh in Ohio Stadium. Three Hungarians were on the team—Csuri, Les Horvath (Ohio State's first Heisman Trophy winner), and Gene Fekete; their fathers found one another and sat together on the sidelines, wearing their sons' numbers over their coats, smoking cigars and talking in Hungarian. When Ohio State took possession of the ball on their own fifteen-yard line, the sons called to their fathers, in Hungarian: "Watch this next play. We're going all the way." They did. They set a Stadium record for rushing eighty-five yards.

Every five years Csuri attends the 1942 team reunions. At least for two days, before they can begin to argue, the aging champions have a wonderful time. They had their forty-fifth reunion in October 1987, when they filed out on the field to be recognized during half time at the Indiana game. "We had to line up a minute or two before the half," Csuri says. "We'd been given instructions on where to stand. There's such intensity on the sidelines. I saw a player running toward our side of the field. And for a split second, I thought maybe, I could do one play."

Once Csuri was on the Ohio State faculty, he developed two remarkable friendships with colleagues. One was an artist; the other, an engineer.

He met Roy Lichtenstein first: the same Roy Lichtenstein who in the early sixties would use comic-strip techniques to become a progenitor of Pop Art. In the late forties Csuri and Lichtenstein, both OSU graduates, both teaching, became cronies. They talked art all the time, they played games with art, they spent evenings looking at pictures in the art library. They sat around cursing Picasso: *He'd done everything.* (What is there to be done is not always easy to see.)

To Csuri, Lichtenstein seemed a sophisticate among the rubes. He was a New Yorker who knew about modern artists, like Paul Klee, whose reputation had yet to cross the Hudson. Csuri, tutorially steeped in Michelangelo, was astonished when in the mid-forties he first saw Lichtenstein doing drawings in the style of Klee; perhaps in recognition of that moment and the leap from provincialism that it presaged, the Lichtenstein work he has in his office today is a Klee-like painting, *The Sheriff.*

After five years on the Ohio State faculty, Lichtenstein was denied tenure in 1951. In spite of the anger Csuri felt at the time, he believes now that Lichtenstein would never have become so famous if he had stayed in Ohio, that he needed the interaction with and encouragement of artists he met later in New Jersey, Allan Kaprow and George Segal. Csuri was amused to see

Lichtenstein, whom the university had in effect fired in 1951, returning in June 1988, for an honorary doctorate.

The engineer was Jack Mitten. Csuri and Mitten became friends in the early fifties. Being a friend, Mitten did buy a couple of Csuri's paintings ("He gave me very good prices"), but what Csuri most talks about now, is how Mitten, a professor of industrial engineering, introduced him to computers in 1955. Over the next decade, they talked often about computers and programming—looking back, Csuri calls it a dialogue.

Csuri found computer graphics in *The Lantern* in 1964. If he had not been talking with Mitten, he would not have been ready to understand what he saw—a *picture* that came from a computer. A device called a Flexowriter had been developed to produce pictures in a computer, which until then could communicate only in letters and numbers. "When I saw you could make pictures," Csuri says, "it just all fell into place for me."

Moreover, if Csuri had been on another campus, it is very unlikely he would have heard of computer graphics so early as 1964; even at that time, he says, OSU was advanced. This picture showed a woman's face in profile. A student in Electrical Engineering's Antenna Lab, J. G. Raudseps, had done his master's thesis on programming gradual shading between the abrupt patches of light and dark gray that the Flexowriter produced. For Csuri, the picture was a revelation: "I knew what I had to do." He started by talking to Raudseps and others in the Antenna Lab. He signed up for a programming workshop on campus. He had to learn how a computer computes and how to tell it what to do. He did not become a particularly skilled programmer (he never did manage a program to convert English pounds into dollars), but he better understood the possibilities. In the next few years as he created art, he produced work that often also credits a programmer, James Shaffer.

Csuri moved into research in the late sixties. In 1970 he

organized seventy-five people to put together an on-campus art show, "Interactive Sound and Visual Systems." Exhibits included four slide projectors whose images could be combined, and computers that let spectators jumble pictures. What the show really did, Csuri says now, was place "the idea of computers in art in front of everybody—particularly in central administration. In hindsight, there's no question it advanced my career." The next year the university provided Csuri a programmer and a computer—and thus gave him the credibility he needed when looking for research money. For the next sixteen years, looking for money was one of his main occupations.

The other was shaping, motivating, and inspiring computer graphics research. He shaped it with a small research group he founded in the late sixties. Thomas Linehan, who joined when he started working on his doctorate in 1972, says the group had a revolving membership of five or six; they included programmers and scientists, artists and designers; they were students, staff, faculty, and always Csuri. Linehan, who took his PhD under Csuri in 1981 and is associate director of ACCAD, says the format, common in science but not in art, was remarkably productive. "There was a kind of shared expertise. You joined the group and assumed responsibility to develop *your* expertise. For example, as software became available, the person familiar with it—often not a professor but a staffer, say—would teach it."

Linehan gives Csuri credit not only for the research format, but also for "highly creative" leadership. "At the time something is being invented," Linehan says, "defining the problem and establishing a direction are tremendously risky." There was even the challenge of selecting the right hardware; for the work to survive, it had to be designed for machines that would survive. Those were the decisions Csuri made.

He was also good at attracting talent, the people who developed the actual technology. They included Tom De Fanti, a student, and professors Frank Crow and John Christian Wedge—now all far-flung leaders in the field. In the 1980s OSU, with one of the top, and easily the biggest, university programs in the country, also became a major source of talent in computer graphics: It granted sixty-five master's degrees and twelve PhDs—eight more were in the pipeline in 1987–88—in the field.

And Csuri brought in the money. He cultivated the clubby national research network. Publicizing what OSU was doing, he became a computer graphics guru, interviewed by Walter Cronkite, appearing on the *Today* show, speaking on panels in New York, California, and Michigan, from a dais at Harvard, at a banquet in Dallas; he made *Business Week, Time, Newsweek,* and television screens all over Europe. It all helped.

For twenty-three OSU projects begun between 1969 and 1987, the money totaled over eight million dollars. Csuri says, "I was very good at getting grants." Much of computer graphics development in the seventies and eighties lies behind project titles like "Real-Time Animation Graphics as a Tool for Research" or "Complex Image Synthesis." The grants were mostly technical. They came from the Navy, the Air Force, and especially from the National Science Foundation, which Csuri says had a "missionary attitude about the computer and wanted to demonstrate it could be used broadly."

When the supercomputer was installed on campus in 1987, its staff and the ACCAD were under one roof: an actual and symbolic interdependence. What's on the mutual agenda are scientific visualizations: pictures to show how natural phenomena—from molecules to hurricanes—work. Because supercomputers process huge quantities of information, such pictures become possible (the machine can handle the horrendous calculations to describe, say, how smoke rises or fluid flows) but also necessary (a ceiling-high stack of numerical printouts is incomprehensible by itself). Starting in 1986 the state and university gave ACCAD five million dollars for five years of supercomputer graphics research. The product, Linehan says, would be "expensive software. There aren't a lot of products that can compete."

In the early eighties, Csuri and Robert Cranston Kanuth, the venture capitalist, became partners in a computer animation company, Cranston/Csuri Productions. An unpaid owner-director, Csuri continued to work for Ohio State during the six years that the company flourished and then collapsed. In the beginning, Cranston-Csuri animations appeared in logos everywhere—on Superbowl programs, in the CBS eye. But if Cranston-Csuri had gone on succeeding, perhaps Csuri wouldn't have come back to making his own art.

In late summer 1988, he scrolls eight pictures, one after another, onto a nineteen-inch screen. He has been thinking about them for months, talking about them. They show skulls, cubes and legless, headless, plaster-like torsos, all floating, casting shadows, covered with paintings. A transparent skull floats in broad, rough stripes of color. Another skull is covered irreverently with doodles; "Still Life" is torsos splattered with fruit—bananas, grapes, melon slices. What he has done is map paintings onto objects; he has selected lighting, perspective, and colors by typing numbers.

He's excited ("Nobody's ever done this before"); he says he's tired of being a research professor; perhaps, he can do this in ("I hate to say this") retirement. "There's a terrible danger of too much gimmickry," he muses. "On the other hand, highly successful artists have a gimmick. Like Lichtenstein—dots are a gimmick. But Lichtenstein has an idea about objects, a wit, an irony. *That* is what artists do.

"What I'm really enjoying is students looking at these and saying, 'Oh, for heaven's sake, why didn't I think of that?'

"Just so long as I don't get too serious. It's the kiss of death."

MARCH CALENDAR

Reflections. In early March, with the fountain still off for the winter, Mirror Lake lived up to its name: On a hazy day the sun's reflection looked like a full moon the color of cream. Nearby, with winter-quarter final exams due to start on the fourteenth, the Main Library was busier than usual. Study tables were all occupied and a perpetual line waited to use the five copying machines on the first floor. Next to a rare-book display, two students took advantage of the carpet to lie down and sleep with their heads on bookbags.

Winning Error. The Press Club of Ohio voted to give its annual Boner Award to Ed Jennings for his role in the firing of Earle Bruce. Even though he won handily, Jennings didn't show up himself to accept his award at the Palace Theatre on March 1. Malcolm Baroway, head of University Communications, went in his place and acknowledged, "There's no question that the situation with the coach and the athletic director made news."

Inn Giving. At their regular meeting, the Board of Trustees voted to accept the gift of the University Inn, a money-losing hotel in need of repairs. Trustee Hamilton J. Teaford cast the only vote against accepting it. He thought it was too risky. President Jennings made it clear that the university had no intention of trying to operate the hotel itself. "Our business is academic," he said.

Pool Games. The first weekend in March at the Big Ten men's swimming championships, Ohio State finished eighth of ten, even though most of the team came in with lifetime bests. "Naturally," said Coach Dick Sloan, "it's disappointing."

Then on the last weekend of the month, the women's synchronized swimming team, perennial winners, placed first in the national collegiate championships. Nine of the fourteen All-Americans were from Ohio State.

Poor Timing. *Lantern* columnist George Vontsolos, a senior, expressed his dismay at being young and lusty in the age of AIDS: "Talk about poor timing. Here I am in my twenty-second year and everyone is fastening their chastity belts." He concluded with a plea for condoms, which "could save lives and, almost as importantly, bring back the dying sexual revolution."

Woody Lives. March 12 was the first anniversary of the death of Woody Hayes. A *Lantern* writer noted that the former coach's name lived on in at least four scholarship programs, the new Athletic Center, and a College of Medicine cancer fund.

Vacation Memos. As spring break approached, sixty-two members of the OSU Men's Glee Club prepared to go on tour; and Carolyn Wesson, a dietician with the Student Health Center, cautioned against crash diets for looking good on a Florida beach. Wesson urged students to lose ten pounds gradually over a whole quarter and not just in the last week.

Winter Commencement. At the university's 303rd commencement on March 18, 1,464 degrees and certificates were awarded to graduates. Speaker and recipient of an honorary degree was Arno Penzias of Bell Labs in New Jersey. A Big

Bang theorist, Penzias was winner of the 1978 Nobel Prize for Physics.

Board Students. In March the Ohio legislature approved appointing nonvoting student trustees to the boards of state universities. Ohio State had officially opposed the bill on the grounds that trustees shouldn't represent special interests.

Greek Surprise. When spring quarter began, students could for the first time sign up for a major in modern Greek. Ten did, which surprised even the professor, Vassilis Lambropoulos. Ohio State, he said, was the second college in the country to offer the major; the other was Queens College in New York. He added that as an academic field, modern Greek was only twenty-five years old.

Pink Floyd for Real. Toward the end of the month, the rumors that Pink Floyd, a British rock group, would play Ohio Stadium turned out to be true. Barry Gabel of Belkin Productions promised that at least 62,000 unobstructed seats would be sold.

Spring for Real. And on the thirty-first, a landscaping tractor was grading the Oval and spreading grass seed.

CHAPTER 7

By Their Hoards Ye Shall Know Them

A mite is a small creature with two body parts and eight legs. It is as small as a speck of dust—in fact, it often is a speck of dust. It evolved on earth 100 million years before insects (three body parts, six legs) and now lives virtually everywhere that life is possible. Although some species have been studied a lot because they are harmful—they can cause Rocky Mountain spotted fever or the itching of scabies—one of the most surprising facts about mites is that so little is known about them.

Thus Warren Calvin Welbourn, Jr., has under the microscope an unknown, unnamed mite of a new genus and species; and only four people on earth have ever laid eyes on it. It is a luminescent white in color and less than half a millimeter long. Now magnified fifteen times, it can be seen to lift and advance a leg, slowly and deliberately. It doesn't have a lot of pep, perhaps because it hasn't eaten for a year. Welbourn did try feeding it—he tried insect eggs and mite eggs, for example—but without success.

As curator of Ohio State's Acarology Collection, Welbourn does know enough about this creature that he will be able to name it. He knows it is a kind of velvet mite—they are one of his specialties. He found this one when it was still a larva, the parasite of a cave cricket, in Alabama. Now it is in an immature stage; if it liked the food here and grew up, it would look the same when it became an adult, only bigger and, at least to others of its ilk, sexier. Welbourn adds that this mite is closely related to one that was found attached to another mite in the stomach of a toad near Hudsons Bay. Straight-faced, he asks, "Do you think I'm making that up?"

Welbourn says that although mites were known to the Greeks, it has been only in this century that there's been much progress in knowing about them. For example, in 1900 fewer than twenty species of chiggers had been named; today there are almost two thousand. But the world is still full of unknown, undiscovered mites—even the immediate world. A couple summers ago, a visiting acarologist from Michigan discovered a new species on the Ohio State campus. Whenever he comes back he makes a point of looking at that tree again. His mite is still living there.

The Acarology Collection is just one of the collections at Ohio State. In fact, it is just one of the university's systematics collections in the natural sciences; it organizes its 150,000 identified specimens by species, genus, and family, which explains how they are related and how they evolved. Because of systematics, Cal Welbourn says, when a 400-million-year-old mite fossil was found in Devonian rock, it could be classified. At Ohio State there are systematics collections of fishes, reptiles, birds, mollusks, mammals, insects (including the biggest aggregation of dead leafhoppers in America), and plants.

The university also has collections of rocks and of old cameras; of rare books, American fiction, medieval Slavic manuscripts, theatrical materials, and cartoons; of OSU telephone books, yearbooks, and photographs; of celebrity eyeglasses; of historic stuff—dental tools, farm equipment, and costumes (including 144 garments from Mrs. Harvey S. Firestone, Jr.);

and of people (represented by their pictures) who have been named to the six halls of fame that somehow cluster here.

Though they are part of Ohio State, these collections are not necessarily scholarly. Halls of fame are obviously promotional, even when they promote a profession people learn at the university. Some, like costumes and rocks, are useful for teaching. But some are emphatically scholarly—like the Acarology Collection, which is deep and particular enough to be a national resource. That leaves the relatively new collection of comics, which is searching for a scholarly identity. Actually, the comics are typical of Ohio State: a populist tradition looking for a little respect.

By and large, the collections are not museums. An exception is the Orton Geological Museum in Orton Hall on the Oval. It's a small museum, so that its Ohio fossils and Ordovician rocks are all accessible; so too the bones of a giant ground sloth found in Holmes County in 1890.

Another collection that anyone may look at is Celebrity Eyewear, which the College of Optometry has established to show that eyeglasses are associated with success. Displayed in cases in the Optometry Clinics hall, the collection is managed by Arol Augsburger, a professor, who himself owns ten or fifteen pairs of glasses. Actually, he wears only four of them regularly; today he is wearing the pair with red frames, which goes with his burgundy tie.

Were it not for the enthusiastic devotion of Augsburger, the Celebrity Eyewear collection would not exist. He is the one who goes through *Time* and *Newsweek* to clip pictures of people with glasses; he is the one who signs the letters that go out in annual batches to bespectacled celebrities—appeals for the old pair of glasses that lie unused in a drawer. Eyeglasses are so expensive, that even celebrities hate to throw them out. "We rely on that," he says.

Since he began amassing the collection in 1983, Augsburger has brought in seventy pairs, which he likes to exhibit with a picture of the celebrity wearing them. Columnist George Will's old glasses are not in the collection; he'd just driven over them. Nor are Senator John Glenn's; he wrote that he so rarely wore his that they weren't part of his public image. But Vice-President Bush sent the pair he was wearing the day Reagan was shot; Ohio Governor Richard Celeste's arrived with scratched lenses; auto racing driver Bobby Rahal's were broken. The few women represented include Sophia Loren and Joan Collins, both of whom are in the frame-designing business, and Miss Piggy, who sent heart-shaped sunglasses with violet frames. Ed Jennings and Earle Bruce both donated glasses, but Augsburger never did get a pair from Woody Hayes. Every time he asked, the former coach would say, "Aw, I'm not a celebrity."

In 1986 the *Los Angeles Times* strayed into the Midwest and found Ohio State's halls of fame, which it wrote about under the headline, SHRINES TO THE OBSCURE FATED TO BLUSH UNSEEN. It is true that few people go out of their way to see these halls of fame, which are located in corridors and rooms around campus. Each one offers a collection of portraits of honorees who tend to be otherwise unknown. By and large they are dull to see but, with their ironic blend of fame and obscurity, wonderful to contemplate. At least that's so for the Accounting Hall of Fame. Thomas J. Burns, the faculty member in charge, thinks the hall should be of interest only to accountants, even though he is "besieged all the time, by writers, by television—could you believe David Letterman? It's not of interest to the public."

The Ohio Journalism Hall of Fame apparently attracts less attention—only a couple calls a year. Founded in 1928, it claims to be the oldest of its type, ahead of Illinois by a few weeks. The Ohio 4-H Hall of Fame honors not 4-H youth whose chickens or lambs were biggest, as might be expected, but volunteers who have served thirty, forty, and even more than fifty years to keep 4-H going. The Ohio State University Sports Hall of Fame does include a few well-known names, like Jesse Owens, Jack Nicklaus, and Archie Griffin. So does the Insurance Hall of Fame, but only by laying claim to comet man Edmond Halley and one-time Chief Justice Charles Evans Hughes.

The Drainage Hall of Fame is the newest and has the best name, resonant with ambiguity. Does it celebrate plumbers? Trickle-down economics? Sewers? Success stories in urology?

It turns out that it's a matter of agricultural drainage, which means getting excess water out of the roots of crops, so that they will grow better or at all. Byron Nolte, a water expert and professor of agricultural engineering, says that, by nature, Ohio was so poorly drained that it was a superb candidate for drainage ditches and subsurface drain-tile pipes. In due course the state became a drainage-industry leader and, Nolte says, Ohio State became "one of the leading, if not the leading, drainage research universities." Thus in 1979, it also seemed the site of choice for the Drainage Hall of Fame for leaders in drainage research, practice, or education.

Of the Ohio State halls of fame, Drainage not only has the best name but also the best display. Since January, 1987, it has occupied a glass case in the lobby of the new Agricultural Engineering Building, where its installation benefitted from the advice of an OSU extension designer, Millie Scheid. Drainage's previous location, a conference room on the second floor of Ives Hall, was, even for an OSU hall of fame, unobtrusive. Scheid describes it: "They had a gray room with a long table and these black-and-white photographs in a row—terrible-looking photos of men. They all looked drained." (In faces, not a virtue.) She decided to make the portraits more contemporary: "I had them photo-etched on gold metal, to give some color to their skin tone, and then I had them mounted on a highly polished gold so it would look like a frame. I put Velcro on the wall so when they add new members they can just pull them off and move them around. We'll be able to get forty people in there." So far, there are only ten faces, smiling and unsmiling, every one an expert on where down is.

As Ohio State collections go, the library must be the Big Daddy, with its millions of everything. The library also harbors six special collections—crannies of scholarship subject to populist intrusions: In Rare Books and Manuscripts *Star Trek* television scripts keep company with one hundred incunabula or books printed before 1501, in the first century of printing. Curator Robert Tibbetts stands in the stacks of his domain, holding a five-hundred-year-old English book. He points out that some words have been crossed out. He thinks that happened in the sixteenth century, when the book had a Protestant owner who crossed out references to the pope and purgatory.

Robert Tibbetts has a broad, pale face ringed in graying hair and beard. In his shirt pocket he keeps three pens (one red), two pencils, a pencil case, a small notebook, and loose papers. He is a third-generation librarian who since 1968 has tended Ohio State's rare manuscripts and printed books, which, besides *Star Trek* and incunabula, include 350 letters from Simone de Beauvoir to Nelson Algren; a large James Thurber collection; Samuel Beckett writings in French and English; and OSU publications. Traffic in Rare Books is steady but low-volume. The item most in demand is not a scholarly one, but rather an OSU publication, the University Personnel Budget. It lists the salaries of every employee.

Humorist James Thurber was a native of Columbus who entered Ohio State in 1913 and attended sporadically for several years, never graduating; to make his reputation, he went to New York. Most of the Thurber material—manuscripts, letters, drawings—came in to Tibbetts, who says he's therefore "referred to as knowing something about Thurber. For much of his life, Thurber had a love-hate relation with the university." In fact when Ohio State offered him an honorary doctorate in 1951, he turned it down because the university was curtailing free speech; OSU, in a McCarthy-era move, was screening campus speakers.

Eight Thurber drawings on plaster are displayed in the Rare-Books reading room (which is officially the James Thurber Reading Room; a plaque says the class of 1917 helped furnish it). The drawings were found under the wallpaper of a Sandy Hook, Connecticut, house where Thurber lived in the early 1930s. In 1977 a conservator removed the plaster, with drawings and even a settlement crack intact. The crack represents a rocky hillside where one man gazes glumly at a bird and another stares malevolently at a flower.

The collection of comics, which is one of the special collections, is entirely populist. It isn't called anything so impish as "comic collection," but rather, the Library for Communication and Graphic Arts. That, says the curator, Lucy Caswell, is "a dreadful name. I always tell people we collect the arts of the mass media." Caswell hopes to build "a comprehensive collection—as much as possible" in cartoon art. No one else has ever done that.

The cornerstone of the collection came from cartoonist Milton Caniff, who graduated from Ohio State in 1930 and went on to create "Terry and the Pirates" and then "Steve Canyon"—two superstars of the funny pages. Caniff (who died April 3, 1988) donated all his papers to this library. "I'm sure," Caswell says, "there's not another collection like Caniff's in the world. We have work dating back to his childhood—we have more than sixty years of his career. We have art work, business files, and forty or fifty thousand fan letters."

The first large shipment of Caniff's work came from his mother's house in Dayton in 1977. With 150 boxes and about nine file cabinets, it was of moving-van proportions, all addressed to Lucy Caswell, who tackled it item by item—"That's how you do what I do." She found everything from a John Steinbeck letter to model airplanes that Caniff used to draw from.

Caswell's only problem is the populist nature of cartoons: In an academic setting, people don't take them seriously enough. So she has thought up research topics that might be explored through cartoons. For example, what do comic strips tell about the role of women? How do political cartoons document historical events? Why is cartoon art such a powerful medium? "I can show you on one hand the serious articles on cartoon art," she laments. But in her quest for respectability, she may be virtually alone. The collection has received original cartoons that had been stuffed into broken window panes, that blotted coffee stains, that served as floormats. Not even cartoonists took the cartoon seriously.

In contrast, the Acarology Collection is entirely scholarly. Not long ago its founder did take a stab at a movie—a crossover to populism—but it didn't work. It may be that although all the world can love a cartoon, only a scholar can love a mite.

The Acarology Collection is not on display. A collected mite is doubly removed: too small to notice and put away besides. If it's been classified, it's probably on a glass slide, where it's a speck in the middle of inscriptions giving its name and the circumstances of its natural habitat. All the rest of the collection is in alcohol in small and large glass jars. As many as a million unsorted mites might be in those jars.

In the United States there are fifty full-time acarologists, and four of them are at Ohio State. Glen Needham, an associate professor, and Dana Wrensch, an adjunct, work mostly with living mites, while Curator Cal Welbourn and Donald Johnston, a professor, concentrate on systematics. For many years Johnston was the curator. He brags now that he's been all over the world building the collection, and he mentions Spanish beech forests ("a marvelous habitat for soil mites") and Mediterranean beaches ("somebody's got to do it") in particular.

"Acarology," Johnston says, "is the study of mites and ticks, keeping in mind ticks are overgrown mites. They are a small arachnid—that's a group of animals that includes spiders and scorpions and daddy longlegs. There are 35,000 named species of mites and there may be half a million in existence. The biggest mites are ticks. There's one that lives on the rhinoceros; the female can get to be an inch long. That's huge. The smallest would be one tenth of a millimeter. For you to see it with the naked eye, it has to be a half millimeter or bigger.

"All animals," Johnston says, "are associated with one or several mite species. Your dog could have two on the skin, one in the ears, one in the nasal passages, and two kinds of ticks. Virtually every person has two species living in their face—follicle mites in the forehead and under the eyes. Most people would not admit to having them. I'm sorry but they're there. And if you consider everyone has mites on their face, then mites are the only animal other than people to go to the moon. Mites are in soil, associated with insects, on plants— that's our bread and butter, the real world. Florida spends fifty million dollars annually to control one citrus mite. And a number of mites live in nests—even *our* nests. House-dust mites live under beds and feed on skin debris or dander. They give some people a house-dust allergy.

"There are mites that would qualify as genuinely beautiful but most of the fascination is anatomical. I work on meso-stigs—that's slang for mesostigmata. This slide from Ottawa was brought to us to see one hair [a sensory seta] on one leg—it's unique to this animal in the mesostig group. I can see the potential reader's suspicions confirmed on what we do at Ohio State—carrying that slide around to look at one hair.

"One of the things that fascinates me is that mesostigs have a unique breathing apparatus. They develop openings in the side of the body which lead to branched tracheae for gas ex-change." At this point Johnston has his arms out at his sides, bent, so that his hands are waving near his ribs to show where mesostigs breathe.

"We have an immense collection," he goes on. "We have diversity and depth. We have the nicest European collection outside of Europe. G. H. Wharton first brought the collection to Ohio State in 1961. It got fair amounts of support from the National Institutes of Health through 1976. After that there was less interest in parasitology. They shifted to allergy or molecular biology."

Johnston says that there are few acarology collections in North America. The Field Museum in Chicago has a large collection; the Smithsonian has one ("It's supposed to be the major collection," he says. "But it doesn't have diversity and depth"). Harvard has a historical collection but no acarologist. Canada has three acarologists to tend its collec-tion in Ottawa.

While there are fifty acarologists in the United States, only two of them are full-time collection curators. One is at the Field Museum, and the other is Cal Welbourn. Welbourn did try living without mites—that is, for seven years he tried teaching high school; but in 1978 he came to the Acarology Collection and began working part time on the doctorate that he got in 1985. As curator he manages the collection and its library and identifies mites people send in. To work with mites, he has small tools. He picks up live ones delicately, with a damp size-zero sable brush. For lifting mites, he has a spatula, custom made in a university workshop: It's a thin, inch-and-a-half-long pin whose point end has been flattened by a machine press.

When mites arrive to join the collection, they may be riding on live mice, rats, insects, birds, bats, reptiles, lizards, snakes, and frogs; or they may be in a clump of grass pulled up roots and all. When Welbourn himself goes out collecting, he is apt to head for the woods and fall to his knees, the better to scoop up forest floor litter. If he's looking for something specific, he'll have his nose to the ground too, so that he can see his prey. Twice—once on his knees in an Italian forest and once in a jarful of Japanese crickets—he has found the second specimen of mites long known by only one example. Three times other researchers have named mite species for Welbourn.

Classifying mites can be complicated. In the summer of 1988 Maria Casanueva, a PhD candidate from Chile, where she teaches at the University of Concepción, was three months into work on her dissertation, which she hoped to finish by summer 1989. She proposed to straighten out classification for a mite family called laelaptidae, which was supposed to include ten genera of soil-dwelling predators and forty-three genera of parasites. "Right now," she said, "the laelaptidae family is really a mess." So for each of the fifty-three genera, she proposed to list seventy characteristics. (Genera can be differentiated by, say, a characteristic like the number of setae on a particular segment of a particular leg.) Then she would pop all the data into the computer, which would spew out orderly groups of laelaptidae.

It sounded simple enough but, she said, "I was just telling Dr. Johnston I am confused. I don't have any conclusions.

Sometimes they're not easy to identify. They could have the wrong name. And it's difficult to define the limits of the family, because you have so much variation in the group. It could be more than one family. Maybe you have to remove some genera and put them in some other family. So far I have at least two species that are in the wrong place. We are putting one of those species in a new genus—that's a paper Dr. Johnston and I are going to publish soon."

She had made fourteen india-ink drawings to illustrate the paper, to show the previously misclassified mite in its various stages of development, with all its setae, pores, muscles, and glands. For just one drawing she had to look at forty-two slides; in its portrait, the adult looked something like a lumpy potato.

That makes it more or less even in beauty with several mites shown in photographic enlargements that Professor Emeritus George Wharton has at his home nearby in Upper Arlington. The house-dust mite looks something like an armadillo; others resemble mounds of corduroy or chenille bedspread. "I think they're beautiful little things," Wharton says.

Wharton is the person who brought acarology to Ohio State. When he arrived in 1961, he had in tow a teaching collection and curator, in the person of Dr. Johnston, and the Acarology Laboratory, a summertime program for advanced students and biologists; when Maria Casanueva first came to Ohio State, before she began her doctorate, she came to attend the Acarology Laboratory. Wharton founded the laboratory at Duke University in 1951, moved it to the University of Maryland in 1953, and thence to Ohio. He retired in 1976 and hasn't had much to do with mites in the last few years, except for the movie.

In the mid-eighties, Wharton had the notion to make a movie about mites—a half-hour video that, in his wildest dreams, would be televised to tell the world about mites and would even bring in enough money to finance a sequel. The first one was about the life cycle of the two-spot spider mite, which lives on plants and leaves webs in its wake. The cast was at hand at Ohio State; Dana Wrensch raises two-spot spider mites, which turned out to be ideal performers. For one thing, they wouldn't walk right off the set. If Wharton put them on a little piece of leaf, they would just stay put and bask in his viewfinder.

In the end, the movie was not a success. It wasn't that the public television and radio station, WOSU, didn't help; they did. They provided a narrator to read Wharton's script. They also did the editing, though it took them a long time to get around to it; Wharton has to admit the project was a pretty low priority for them. What really confounded him, though, was the music. He thought orchestral music in the background would help the movie through the duller stages in the life cycle of the two-spot mite, but "it was a thousand dollars for eighteen seconds or some outlandish thing." So Wharton went to another OSU collection—the Borror Laboratory of Bioacoustics, which has 21,500 recorded animal sounds—and asked for the most musical ones on hand. Thus, for a dramatic high point like the emergence of the larva from the egg, the film's background music is a combination of a cicada chorus and woodthrush at half speed. Wharton finds it interesting but not quite right. "I probably should have gone to the music department."

APRIL CALENDAR

Money Returns. On Tuesday, April 5, the wind blew away hot-dog man John Murphy's money. It happened in mid-afternoon, when Murphy was only in his fourth day of running a hot-dog stand on the Oval. A sudden gust slammed the pushcart umbrella onto his hand—the hand that was holding all the day's receipts. The money flew off "like leaves in the wind," he said later. "It scattered all over the northeast quadrant of the Oval. A girl was standing here and she yelled at the people she was with and they ran after the money. Other people were lying on blankets and they grabbed money as it was blowing by. Within two minutes as many as twenty students returned with money, some from as far as a hundred yards away, and I had a bagful of bills all crumpled up with leaves and grass."

When he counted it at the end of the day, Murphy—who would have been responsible for any losses—found all the money was there in the bag. "I didn't lose anything," he said. "It was amazing." He wrote a letter to *The Lantern* commending the honesty of students.

Board Matters. At its regular monthly meeting on April 8, the Board of Trustees agreed to make structural improvements in St. John Arena, which had been off-limits for rock concerts since the mid-seventies, when a study showed harmonic vibrations could weaken the building. Agricultural administrator Frederick Hutchinson reported that OSU researchers and Smucker's, the jam manufacturer, were working on a genetically perfect jam strawberry. And when an Undergraduate Student Government spokesman thanked the university for permitting the upcoming Pink Floyd concert, Trustee Deborah Casto pointed out that "the concert is not just for the students."

Workers Settle. The OSU chapter of the Communications Workers of America ratified a new three-year contract with the university on April 10. The union's 2,500 service and skilled workers were promised annual raises and an increase in the square footage cleaned by union custodians rather than by contract services.

OSU Elects. Eight teams of presidential and vice-presidential candidates vied in the USG's annual election Wednesday and Thursday, April 13 and 14. Two weeks later—after an investigation into improper campaign practices, such as putting posters in the wrong places—OSU computers processed the 4,565 ballots. Winners were Athena Yiamouyiannis, president, and her running mate, Scott Mounts.

Seen Passing. Campus events included an April 13 forum, "Covert Action: Is It Necessary?" co-sponsored by Students for Peace and Justice; a speech by West Germany's former chancellor, Willi Brandt on the eighteenth; an appearance the next day by labor activist Cesar Chavez, who spoke on "The Wrath of Grapes"; and a primary campaign appearance by Vice-President George Bush on April 30.

Any Time Is Football Time. When Coach John Cooper got a look at the football Buckeyes at spring practice, he said that he was not at all sure he could do better than Earle Bruce had with these players. "I really think we had better talent the last two or three years at Arizona State than they've had at Ohio State," he said. "That's the most disappointing thing I find here." Between the new coach and spring practice, the autumn sport of football was getting more coverage in April *Lanterns* than any OSU sport except baseball—more than in-season men's and women's track, tennis, and golf combined.

Buckeye Dedication. Before the annual intra-squad game April 30, three new trees in the Buckeye Grove were dedicated to Ohio State's latest crop of All-Americans. Of the honorees, Tom Tupa was away but Chris Spielman turned out as did Cris Carter, who, ineligible to play for OSU in 1987 (he had accepted money from an agent), had turned pro and played for the Philadelphia Eagles. Spielman was casual in warm-up sweats but Carter's clothes were fancy—an elegant olive suit.

A small crowd attended the ceremony and heard short speeches from a visibly moved Spielman ("This is a bittersweet time for me") and from Carter (introduced as "the premier receiver in the history of this university," he said, "I know God has forgiven me and I'd like you to do that also"). After the ceremony, a gray-haired spectator said, "That was nice, wasn't it?" and he took off his glasses to wipe an eye. On the ground, next to their respective saplings, the three new plaques, shaped like Ohios, glittered in the sunlight.

One of the people there was Carter's erstwhile roommate, football player William White, who the previous week had been a fourth-round draft pick of the Detroit Lions. He said he'd already been up to Detroit and found he could continue his metallurgical engineering studies there on a part-time basis. He hoped to come back to Ohio State to graduate.

The crowd that turned out for the intra-squad Scarlet and Gray game afterward was the largest ever—54,302 people. John Cooper was again surprised: "To have this many people come for a spring scrimmage is unbelievable. The fan support here is unreal."

CHAPTER 8

The Bee Shoot, a Sheep Named Canasta, and Other Job Stories

The Ohio State University employs about seventeen thousand people. Some of them have jobs that are unusual, if not downright odd. Teaching and research at times have peculiar needs, leading to jobs that are intrinsically odd or become so. Also, having an airport and hospitals, living facilities, roads, buildings and farms, OSU has many people in jobs—such as aircraft attendant, surveyor, boat operator—that aren't expected at a university. The very array of jobs in this one institution is extraordinary. Here are people who feed chickens, faculty, and bats, who repair heart-lung machines, boilers, and cars, who run nuclear reactors and cash registers.

Ohio State has on its payroll a Japanese language library cataloguer and a woman who feigns symptoms of illness to train medical students. It has a horticulturist who grows only medicinal plants—an unusual job because medicinal gardens are rare; Americans prefer to do research in synthetic pharmaceuticals because they're easier to patent. So says Karen Chernesky, who does medicinal gardening—an outdoor plot and an indoor greenhouse—for the College of Pharmacy. Because she grows "restricted plants," the greenhouse—which is off the third floor of Parks Hall—is hard to find, though at the moment the restricted vegetation is just four little marijuana plants in large pots.

Ohio State can provide all kinds of unexpected job opportunities. Ask Herb Asher. He started out as merely a professor of political science, but now he's also a player; he's part of the process of politics. Since 1983, on a half-time basis, he's been "the only formal university lobbyist." His stomping ground is the state legislature; his goal, to promote the university budget and autonomy. It is a Tuesday in October as Asher talks about this, and he is interrupted by a call from a state senator's office. They want eight tickets for Saturday's football game. Field seats are all that are left; Asher warns the caller these seats are low, with little visibility. "Everybody is frustrated by being in the ticket business," he says afterward. The call is the first of three such requests in an hour. That reminds him of the other drawback to being a lobbyist: "Working at football games. I've had to get dressed up for games, wear a tie. A faculty member doesn't have to do that. I often think of my old slovenly ways."

Sometimes it is not so much the job that is unusual, as the way it is filled. Pat Stewart is a telephone operator. But with half the Ohio State phonebook in her head, she is no ordinary operator. She takes a call: "Ohio State University . . . Sure. Call 292-4843. They asked for the computer center. When you give a number fast, people will ask, 'How did you know that?' I've always picked up on numbers. I have quite a few in my head. Ohio State University . . . Sure. Call 292-1631. That's Raney Commons. At home I've only answered the phone 'Ohio State University' once. The Ohio State University . . . Sure. 293-8181. She called for magnetic resonance. One time Mike, my husband, and I were driving around campus and I said, 'There's the math building: 4975. There's engineering: 2651. There's Denney Hall: 6065.' He told me to shut up.

"The Ohio State University . . . Sure. The number's 4444. That's the state 4-H office. How do you like that, four 4s? Technically our job is just phone numbers. But sometimes we help people who are lost. Or people call and ask how to spell words, like *sincerely*. I had a guy phone from out of town and ask where would be nice to take a girl. Of course, I asked what he wanted to spend. People call and ask where to live— I sent a guy from Arizona the housing ads from *The Lantern*.

"People want to know what our colors are. Did you ever try describing scarlet over the phone? I tell them it's red. The Ohio State University . . . 292-5731 . . . You're welcome. That was the medical bookstore. Once during the football season a man called from California to ask where he could get buckeyes for his girlfriend. I kept him on hold and called around. I found some at College Traditions and gave him the number. We get calls from overseas. Late one afternoon a man from Australia told me it was the next morning. You think that didn't make me tired?"

In half an hour Pat Stewart had to look up just two numbers: dairy science and the extension of a professor whose baby sitter was locked out.

Like telephone operator, the job that Bunny Clark has— physics professor—is the kind of job a university is expected to have. But just as Pat Stewart fills her job in an unusual way, so too is Bunny Clark an unusual physics professor. Before the 1980s, Ohio State had never had a woman assistant, associate, or full professor of physics. Since 1981 it has had each at least once, because of her: She was first again, again, and again. She has an office on the fourth floor of Smith Lab—a businesslike office with two keyboards and two terminals (both hooked up), a bookcase (*Subatomic Physics, Particles and Nuclei, Relativistic Dynamics and Quark-Nuclear Physics*), and a poster from Hawaii on the wall. She is tall, her gray hair is swept into a French roll, and she has an OSU pin on the flamboyant blue scarf that she wears at her neck.

"In 1969 I had been working for General Motors Research

Lab and was finishing my PhD at Wayne State in Detroit when my husband's business moved to Columbus," she says. "I walked into Ohio State off the street and the chairman hired me as a research associate. Also, I was allowed to use the computer for my own research. I finished my PhD in 1973 and in 1980 the Physics Department advertised for someone in my field. I applied and joined the faculty as an assistant professor. In six years, I became a professor. Once I got on, I did all right." There are fifty faculty in physics, she says, and she has by now been joined by a second woman. Still, she is one of only three female full professors in the College of Mathematics and Physical Sciences, which altogether has sixteen women faculty and 230 men.

For a woman born in 1935, as Bunny Clark was, becoming a physicist was an improbable destiny. Clark thinks she is one of only four nuclear physicists who are women now in their late forties and fifties. She first studied physics in high school in Manhattan, Kansas (the teacher was "Old Ruler Smile") and majored in it at Kansas State University. Her professors suggested she become a science librarian.

As a research associate at Ohio State in the early seventies, Clark says, "I did things like make display cases. I was advising undergraduate physics majors. I taught a few courses— the 130 series in engineering physics. I spent a lot of time with Bernard Mulligan and Leonard Jossem designing a course for nonscience majors—Physics 100; I taught that.

"And I used the computer—the research I do is very computer intensive. It involves a particular approach to understanding the atomic nucleus in the framework of Einstein's special theory of relativity. For fifty years in nuclear physics people believed you didn't have to consider relativistic effects, that Newton's laws were sufficient. Well, I started working on aspects of that in the early seventies. At the time there were very few people doing that—a group at Stanford, a group at the University of Florida, and the Ohio State group, which consisted of me. Now eleven or twelve percent of the field is working in this area—today our OSU group includes two faculty, four post-docs, and three graduate students.

"As a research associate, I was doing things faculty were doing—I was researching and publishing, doing service and teaching; but if a person is doing faculty work they should be eligible for tenure and I wasn't. People might have perceived this as discrimination. Maybe the department was told it would be in the university's best interest to avoid an affirmative action complaint, and the easiest way was to drop my research, service, or teaching. Anyway, they asked me to stop teaching. I was very unhappy. I complained.

"But from 1975 on I wasn't teaching, though my research started to be noticed in 1978 or 1979. I became a senior research associate and then a senior research scientist. When they started advertising for an assistant professor in the winter of 1980, I applied. Even then they offered the position to someone else first, but he took a job at the University of Massachusetts. Physics is very competitive. There just aren't many openings. You have to be willing to compete essentially against men all the time for funds, recognition, students. You don't want to be a pushy broad. But no one will do it for you.

"Until this year there were two bathrooms on this floor, both men's rooms. But there were three women faculty and graduate students, and four word-processing specialists, all going down to the third floor or usually up to astronomy on the fifth floor. We all signed letters. It took a concerted effort to get them to change." She's talking about a fourth-floor men's room in Smith Lab that at the beginning of winter quarter, 1988, got a hand-lettered LADIES ROOM sign and a three-panel screen to block off the urinals. The screen was covered with pictures—impressionist prints, a moose in Yellowstone Park, and the Statue of Liberty.

133

*   *   *

If physicist was an unlikely occupation for Bunny Clark, so was glassblowing for Bill Henthorne. Glassblowing sounds so quaint and archaic—which is not how you'd describe Bill Henthorne. After a stint in the service during World War II, he originally thought he might study horticulture at OSU. "My girlfriend was the daughter of the head glassblower here at Ohio State," Henthorne says. "I used to go down and watch him work in his basement—most glassblowers have their own small business. I'd have a date with Kathleen and wind up in the basement for three hours. It was love at first sight. He'd show me how to blow bulbs, bend tubing, seal tubing together, make condensers—one tube inside another. What you could do with glass was so intriguing.

"When a position opened here, he suggested I apply. They hired me as an apprentice when I was nineteen, and fourteen years later I was managing the department. Most major universities—all the Big Ten schools—have glassblowers. Seventy-five percent of our work is for chemistry, and the rest is strung out over campus—engineering, the vet clinic, the hospital. I like to make new glassware—something that's never been made before. I can give a researcher an estimate if a plan will work. 'Sir, if we change this, it'll work.' Without experience you couldn't imagine what he's trying to do.

"I retired once in 1978 when I was fifty-three and then came back—the young man I had trained went into wine sales. They reinstituted my vacations and allowed my son Tim a tuition discount. I've been back over four years. I have four children. [Kathleen and Bill Henthorne were married in 1949.] Tim's the youngest. He's working for me as a student laborer. He's majoring in photography but he's learning to do this. It's a father-son thing."

Henthorne holds a one-inch glass tube in a flame until a segment is red. Then he corks the tube at one end and blows into the other until the red area balloons out, the beginning of a flask. "Just feel the heat coming off that," he says. "I always tell people I'm not going to hell because I can take the heat."

A university is not expected to have an airport, but then Ohio State has never been limited to normal expectations. It does have an airport, which is almost eight miles north of the main campus. Called Don Scott Field, it is at the center of a three-square-mile university complex that includes cornfields and livestock facilities and is set incongruously in the middle of northwest Columbus, the city's fastest-growing sector.

The airport—named for Captain Don Scott, OSU's starting quarterback from 1938 to 1940 and later an aviator who was killed on duty in England during World War II—is a general aviation facility with a building where pilot logbooks and OSU T-shirts are for sale. There is also a little restaurant, the Barnstormer, whose walls are cluttered with pictures of airplanes. Like many small airports, this one is raffish and romantic.

Given the airport, Ohio State employs a man to maintain runways. He is Richard Lyle ("known as Gus. A slew of people don't know I've got any other name") Custer. He says that Don Scott Field, with 160,000 takeoffs and landings, is the fifth busiest airport in Ohio. Three hundred fifty private aircraft are based here. So are the OSU flight team and the university's airplanes: fourteen trainers and two cabin class (one owned, one rented). The airport has four runways plus taxiways. Custer pulls out one of his cards, which has a little map of the runways: The two parallels and two crosswinds look like a Roman numeral ten. "All the runways are one hundred feet wide," he says. "The longest is five thousand feet. We've had a TWA 707 land but that was not planned.

"Runways are built usually to heavier specifications than

roads. Ours are ten inches of asphalt, which was put down in 1972. We've put slurry over it—that's asphalt and aggregate; we don't dare let it get to potholes. And we get upset if we get stones on the runway—a rock can damage a propellor or tear up fans turning at fifty thousand rpm in a jet engine. We want bare, dry pavement no matter what. We have a rotary broom sixteen feet long and twenty-two-foot snowplows. We plow, sweep, and blow snow—we have to lob it way out in the field. We can't have piles more than one foot high next to the runway because airplane wings will hit it.

"With your car you can slow up for snow or ice but a plane has to land at, say, a hundred knots. So we use sand and urea, which is forty-five percent nitrogen fertilizer and melts the ice. You can't use salt because it will corrode your aircraft and rust out the bolts holding it together. But the urea fertilizer runs off onto the grass along the runway. You have to mow the hell out of it in the spring.

"All runway pavement is striped and all the marks mean something. Runway marks are white and taxiway marks are yellow. Once a year we paint. Campus has a crew of painters who are frantic doing parking lots and roads when students aren't around in summer; then they come up here in September."

It is late afternoon in August, and Gus Custer gives a tour of the airport. He points out the urea and sand stockpiles, the control tower, the new catch basins, the sheds for the immense runway-maintenance trucks. He is driving a yellow pickup truck with "15" painted on the sides; the radio is tuned to the control tower, which calls him "Truck One-Five." He waits ("Truck One-Five hold short of two-seven left") for three small planes to land before he gets clearance to turn onto the runway; then for a few minutes, this wingless yellow craft owns two-seven left. Gaining speed, it streams toward the horizon at thirty-five miles per hour, for all the world as if about to take off.

Just across the road from the airport is the bailiwick of Gus Custer's fellow OSU employee, Ron Guenther, who is a shepherd. Airplanes often fly over the sheep facilities, but for the three hundred ewes and lambs outside in large pens, airplanes are not so interesting as Ron Guenther's pickup truck. Unlike Custer's, which glides on immaculate runways, Guenther's pickup bounces along on gravel; it attracts baaing flocks that trot out and cluster expectantly along the fences.

Being a modern shepherd, Guenther has an office. In a corner of the barn, it has a concrete floor, flies, magazines like *Suffolk Banner* and *Dorset Journal*, and envelopes from OSU campus mail. Plaques for prize animals cluster on the walls, along with a sheep-and-wool map of the world and two crooks, one of which, he says, served for decades as a prop at the old Metropolitan Opera House in New York.

"Very few sheep get through this facility without being used by a student," Guenther says. "We feel we should have as much hands-on as possible, because ninety-five percent of our students have no livestock background anymore. They don't know how to catch a sheep underneath the chin—at first kids tend to grab by the throat and not under the jaw—or by the flank where there's not much wool. You don't like to pull on wool. It bruises.

"Animal Science 500, which is a judging course, comes here, and Animal Science 200, but the basic course is Sheep Production. Nutrition. Breeding. Genetics. Trim the feet, drench for parasites, dock the tails, castration—we castrate two thirds of the male lambs and sell them for meat."

Half the OSU sheep are Dorsets, the subject of research because they will breed out of season and ultimately may produce a year-round lamb supply. A quarter of the flock are Hampshires; and a quarter are Suffolks descended largely from thirty donated in 1977 by LeDale Weiche, a New York editor who had been raising them on her Connecticut farm. "She'd been having trouble keeping help," Guenther says. "The place had to be immaculate and the sheep were babied. Each had its name. Monopoly. Cribbage. Charades. Gin. Roulette, Canasta, and Hopscotch. She knew all these ewes by their names. They even came to their names. She'd invited her friends up from New York City for a coming-out party for Jogger, her new ram. The average livestock person has trouble understanding that."

When Weiche despaired of keeping people to care for her flock in the proper style, she gave them to Ohio State—along with the crook from the Metropolitan Opera—but she did not lose interest in her Suffolks. Until she died in the early 1980s, Guenther says, "A couple times a year she'd come in for a day or two and visit. I'd often call to tell her how they were doing, and I'd have to have a key with their numbers and names in front of me. She gave us donations so we could keep improving them. Once we paid ten thousand dollars for a ram and once we sold one for twenty thousand.

"We did have to handle them differently because they'd been babied so much. It's highly unusual to have sheep come when you call them by their name. I'm not sure they even realized they were sheep."

When Guenther started working at Ohio State in the sixties, the sheep facility was on west campus. One day then Coach Woody Hayes, in the course of one of his legendary walks, strode into the pasture where Guenther was working, and the two of them spent the morning talking. "He was interested in why I mated certain rams to certain ewes," Guenther recalls. "At the end he said most of his top athletes had mothers who were athletically inclined. He said, 'I'd have a helluva team if I could pick the sires and dams of my players.'"

In the line of work one afternoon, a photographer and an editor put on light-colored clothing and went to get pictures of a professor who said he would have bees swarm on his arm. As jobs go, photographer and editor are fairly common. But at Ohio State, the institution shapes common jobs and their possibilities.

Kevin Fitzsimons has a job as an OSU photographer. He claims the photographers "probably see more of the university than any single office. We cover asbestos removal, Pink Floyd, football and basketball games, visiting dignitaries, check-passings—dinners for donors. We do interesting photos of people cutting lawns, sunsets on Gibraltar Island, welding engineering—that's fun, because the sparks are flying. We run into problems, such as one guy who is proud of not having been photographed for a long time. Maybe a hundred times a year we do pictures of Dr. Jennings. He's one of the easiest to deal with. He knows a good photograph is good PR. Now I'm working on a physics brochure. I photographed a lecture—'Light-Cone Wave Functions for Hadrons and Nuclei.' I have no idea what that was. They wanted to show we bring in world-famous people. Probably the most bizarre was liver transplants—we call it a 'liver harvest.' It was 2 A.M. on a Saturday morning."

Sandi Rutkowski has a job as an editor. She works for the College of Biological Sciences, and one of her projects is the annual *Synergy*, a twenty-eight-page magazine with a full-color cover and articles on researchers in the college. In the fall of 1988, *Synergy* had a record press run of thirteen thousand copies distributed mostly to alumni, but also to administrators, press, interested researchers. What Rutkowski does, she says, is "pick the theme, interview and write, work with the photographer, select the photos, and chew my fingernails." Once she thought she would be a film reviewer, but then in graduate school in journalism at Ohio State in 1980, she took science writing, which has pretty well shaped her life.

She has been cleaning her office, a former ladies' lounge with painted cinderblock walls; it is a windowless hole ("I'd kill for a window") in the almost windowless Biological Sciences Building. Cleaning is one of her rituals before she sits down to write. "You sharpen pencils, sort pens, make sure you have M & Ms on hand and sort them by color. You call everyone you know to tell them not to call for several weeks. Writing is so much like giving birth—the pregnancy, the long, very protracted labor period, and then you just hope you have a beautiful child you can be proud of and show off and say, 'Look, at last!'

"Sometimes I do thirty-two drafts. I have to do drafts and let them sit for a while. It's the only way I can get enough distance to edit my own work. The trick is not to get so much distance that it's coming at me as if out of someone else's life. I had to learn to be relentless with myself. I used to be mortally offended if someone got too free with the red pen. Now I find myself shredding things and starting over.

"I try a lot of things to free up what's there. Yesterday I took a long walk and when I came back I worked on nine stories. I'm really into clothes. When I'm feeling lousy I wear a bright-red vintage dress that gets me back. I never dress too casually—that has a detrimental effect. I'm not sure I could write in my navy-blue suit. It might be too rigid. It's good for receptions. I have my OSU logo pin on it.

"When I first started I would agonize over a cover. Somehow I stopped thinking about them and they happen. This week I interviewed Rob Page, who studies bee behavior. We were talking about photographs and he said he can get bees to do all sorts of neat tricks. He said, 'I can have five or six pounds of bees hanging off my arm.' At that point I got a vivid picture in my mind of being outside with a blue sky and this guy standing there with these bees on his arm. I saw a cover."

Thus on the afternoon of Tuesday, May 31, a warm, sunny day when the sky was blue, Sandi Rutkowski and Kevin Fitzsimons are just doing their jobs when they meet Rob Page at the Bee Lab to take pictures, one of which, Rutkowski hopes, will end up as a cover for *Synergy*. The lab is in a converted farmhouse whose white paint is peeling; the location, in back of the Woody Hayes Athletic Center, is a small island of trees and overgrown grass to which Rutkowski attributes "a certain seedy charm."

Page has primed the bees by feeding them sugar water for twenty-four hours; that, the warm weather, and the generally abundant supply of nectar should combine to make them relatively agreeable. Page explains that the object will be to get the bees to swarm on his arm. To attract them, he will hold the queen, which is in a cage the size of a cigar. Page says he learned stunts like this from Norman Gary, his professor at the University of California at Davis and "the best bee behaviorist in the world." Hollywood has often hired Gary to do killer-bee movies.

Even though the bees are expected to be good-natured, Page has told Rutkowski and Fitzsimons to wear light-colored clothes because dark colors attract bees. Page warns: "If a bee walks up your pants leg stomp them out." For a while the bees fly around and then gradually swarm not on Page's arm but twenty feet overhead where another queen evidently has lodged in a tree. "We're lucky to have any bees at all," Page says. "They could have all been gone." A post-doc comes out of the lab and shakes the branch; a cloud of frantic bees fills the air. Rob Page is calling them—"Back down here boys"— and offering his arm. "It's a huge swarm. If I could even get half . . ."

This time they do find Page and his queen. "We need a shot with all these wings glittering in the sunlight," Rutkowski says. "I'm working on it," Fitzsimons says. He is taking pictures continuously—he has two cameras, one with black-and-white film; one with color. The first bees cluster on Page's hand; as more join, the swarm extends up his forearm. "They kind of scratch," Page says. "They tug at the hairs. This is one heavy glove." Five pounds of bees—that's seventeen thousand insects—are on his arm, crawling up to his shoulder, ready to fly into his mouth when he talks. Rutkowski is delighted: "That's a *nice* swarm. It's amazing. Great."

When Fitzsimons has enough pictures, Page shakes the swarm off his arm and hangs the cage with the queen on a low tree branch. He has trouble attaching it and his thumb lands on a bee that stings him—the only sting of the day.

Fitzsimons packs up his gear, pulls off the light-colored sweatshirt he's been wearing, and hoists his camera bag onto his hip. He says that for an OSU photographer, this was a typical assignment—though "being outside was a break."

MAY CALENDAR

Jackson Rally. On Monday, May 2, the night before the Ohio primary, Jesse Jackson spoke to eleven thousand people at St. John Arena. The rally was a success, but the next day Michael Dukakis outpolled Jackson four to one.

Excess Leisure. "Who said life isn't going to have its hits?" Earle Bruce, unemployed football coach, was having coffee at a Bob Evans restaurant May 4. He was tanned from playing golf and traveling around to watch spring practices—he'd been to Brigham Young, the University of Michigan, Notre Dame, Georgia, and others. All in all, though, he'd had more time than he really needed. He'd had time to clean the basement, plant flowers, cook ("stir-fried stuff," bananas Foster, fruit salad for his grandson), and "probably get on the family's nerves. I don't like sitting around. I like coaching. That's my life. I can do a good job for someone. Look at the record—hey, I'm a winner."

Toward the end of June Bruce was offered a job at the University of Northern Iowa and he signed immediately.

Dearer OSU. At the trustees meeting May 5 President Jennings proposed tuition hikes for the next year, from $630 to $680 a quarter for Ohio residents. He coupled that with a plea for ongoing state support to hold tuition down: "A fundamental principle of Ohio State's land-grant mission is accessibility." An editorial ran in *the Lantern* opposing increases, but otherwise objections were muted.

Honors. Thirty-seven students were initiated into Mortar Board, an honorary society, in a midday ceremony at the Browning Amphitheater May 11. Before the ceremony Ed Merta, Jr., a student from Vandalia ("a sheltered suburban paradise") tended the table where candles, scrolls, and framed certificates waited. Mostly, he was holding things down in the wind. When at 12:30 the procession of white-robed initiates and black-robed members began, everything they needed for the ceremony was still on the table.

News Items. In May a program to provide two mentors—one faculty or staff and one student—for black freshmen entering in the fall was announced.

Rich Parks, the 1987 drum major, outscored five challengers in try-outs on the twentieth. Each performed the traditional ramp entrance, the "Buckeye Battle Cry," and other routines.

And on the sixteenth Gay and Lesbian Awareness Week got underway with an appearance by Pat Parker, a black lesbian feminist poet, who read from her works in the law auditorium.

Scoreboards. Of the sports whose seasons ended in May, women's golf had the best finish: first in the Big Ten. It was OSU's only Big Ten first all year, though the lacrosse team tied for first in its Great Lakes Conference. The softball team finished seventh of seven, but four of its players made the Academic All Big Ten.

Two men qualified for Olympic trials in track: Joe Greene in the triple jump and Roget Ware in the 110-meter high hurdles. Two women also qualified: Bridgette Tate, in the 200-meter dash and 100-meter hurdles, and long jumper Theresa Diggs, who on May 21 at Ann Arbor set a Big Ten record of 20 feet 11¾ inches.

Death and Life. Serious matters of death and life intruded. Early in the morning of Friday, May 13, a twenty-one-year-old art major died in his dormitory room of an overdose of drugs or alcohol, or both: an apparent suicide. He was remembered as an accomplished filmmaker. Then at 3:21 A.M. on May 24, an eighteen-year-old student gave birth in the Morrill Tower restroom. She was taken to University Hospitals; the baby, who was five weeks premature but in stable condition, to Children's Hospital. Police said no one but the student knew she was pregnant.

Prize Writing. On May 21 writing awards were announced at a reception in the Faculty Club. Nine graduate and undergraduate poets, fiction writers, and essayists received prizes named for their benefactors and in amounts of from one hundred to one thousand dollars. Only the prize that English major Susan Luke received—two hundred dollars for the best undergraduate poem—was unnamed. The donor was a member of the university maintenance staff who wanted to remain anonymous.

Two Concerts a Day. On Saturday afternoon, May 28, former students of William Baker, for twenty-five years a professor of oboe and English horn, came from all across the United States to mark his imminent retirement with a concert. Five-hundred people heard six oboes, six English horns, six bassoons and contra bassoons, and two flutes (flutists who also played piccolo) perform Percy Grainger's 1901 composition, "Hill Song No. 1." The piece is so rarely performed that Baker said, "I know of no one else who's ever done it."

That night, in another unprecedented event, 63,000 people turned out at Ohio Stadium to hear Pink Floyd. Some football fans had protested that the concert would defile the stadium; one harassed staffer complained, "You'd think it was the first rock concert in the Vatican." Mary Basinger, Ed Jennings's secretary, said she had bought a ticket; and though Jennings's son would be going, they hadn't been able to talk the president himself into it.

Though more than a thousand ticket holders were still in line for alcohol, drug, camera, and tape-recorder searches, the concert began at nine and then was audible for blocks around. Indeed, a mile and a half away, William Baker, who that afternoon had at last heard "Hill Song No. 1" done properly, sat in his backyard and listened to Pink Floyd. By the end of the evening, there had been twenty-five arrests—a few more than usual at a football game—and net profits for the university came to $135,464. Some was set aside to promote more popular concerts.

CHAPTER 9

The Top of the Chart

For President Edward H. Jennings, Wednesday, May 11 begins with a 7:30 breakfast at the Ohio Union's Terrace Dining Room. When he arrives, he helps himself to yogurt and fruit rather than hot sausage and eggs, and then sits with five students at a round table. This is a student breakfast—about thirty of them are here, plus a scattering of staffers. As the meal devolves to coffee, Jennings stands and, to explain the occasion, says, "The institution is large but we try to make it small." Then, for about an hour, he answers questions.

The students see the vintage Jennings—agreeable, never at a loss for words, deft with answers direct and, when he doesn't have first-hand knowledge of a situation, indirect. He is familiar with retirements in the Veterinary School, federal support for financial aid, who runs AT&T (arts and humanities graduates). He says, "For the last fifty years I would match Ohio State's *senior* class against any senior class in the country." And, "Ohio State can no longer afford to be all things to all people." And, when a student asks about crisis planning, "The crisis we can predict won't ever be a crisis; I can virtually guarantee that three weeks from now during exam period we'll get some bomb threats." More than once he compliments his audience; he tells them he will learn from

147

their questions. That is true. He learns also from a lack of questions: No one asks about the proposed tuition hike.

He mentions this afterward, walking across the Oval to his office with an aide, Barbara Tootle. At the breakfast she took notes on all the questions, including the complaints—a department that never answers its phones, or a college with "pitiful" honors advising. Jennings talks about questions he fielded the day before in Elyria, where he spoke to the Rotary Club. "One man asked about athletic issues," he says. "I bet he was trying to get at the Earle Bruce thing." As part of OSU's settlement with Bruce, Jennings agreed not to discuss the firing, so he routinely deflects any questions. But even on a warm and sunny May morning, "the Earle Bruce thing" is a perhaps diminished but persistent cloud over his shoulder.

The president's office is on the second floor of Bricker Hall. The stairs to his office are equipped with riot gates, relics of the 1970 turbulence that shut down the university. These days, the gates are folded back, but they give ongoing testimony to the significance of the office. With the Board of Trustees, the president is at the top of that 128-box university organization chart, which covers everything OSU does, wherever it does it in this multi-campus, multi-faceted, and far-flung (from the likes of Lake Erie's Gibraltar Island to the Molly Caren farm near London, Ohio) domain. Not only does the president have to administer Ohio State's activities in all these places, but he also has to formulate and promulgate the governing ethic, the motive, the philosophy. One hallmark of this administration is that the organization chart itself is perennially tentative. The institution is not supposed to be *finalized*.

Jennings is a lean man with a large head and fine brown hair, with prominent brown eyes and oversized gold-rimmed glasses; he talks in the gravelly basso profundo that only a smoker can perfect. He is typical of university presidents.

Born February 18, 1937, he is near the average age of fifty-three; he is white and male; he has a doctorate (from the University of Michigan in finance); early in his academic career he moved onto an administrative track. In 1979 he left a post as vice-president for finance at the University of Iowa to take the presidency of the University of Wyoming, which is where Ohio State found him when it was looking in 1981.

"The faculty," Jennings says, "are the most important people on campus." He is himself a member of the faculty; he teaches an undergraduate class in beginning finance, though not every quarter. Like everyone else on the faculty, Jennings has an "A" parking sticker—he chooses not to pull rank (even on this campus whose parking problem he describes as insoluble) by having his own parking space.

By and large, Ohio State's faculty have returned the esteem he professes for them. They liked the way he pulled Ohio State out of the financial quagmire it was in when he arrived, when even tenured jobs were in jeopardy. They liked the way he promptly convinced the trustees to drop a loyalty oath, a vestige of the McCarthy era that hung on into the eighties. Faculty had to swear they were not Communists bent on overthrowing the government of the United States or even that of Ohio. William Protheroe, an astronomy professor, says there's little doubt the oath hampered faculty recruiting.

Many of the faculty admired the way Jennings handled the South African divestment issue, which tore some U.S. campuses apart. When OSU protestors called on the university to oppose apartheid by selling all its stock in companies doing business in South Africa, in early 1985 Jennings appointed a committee of fourteen students, staff, and faculty who represented all points of view on divestment. Appointee Marshall Swain, a philosophy professor, says that in the end a committee majority favored immediate total divestment. A minority favored continued investment in companies that followed the

Sullivan Principles, which proposed that companies might influence South African reform. "Jennings," says Swain, "adopted a policy that was in my opinion a genuine compromise: The university would completely divest itself, but it wouldn't do so immediately." (Swain adds that, in an ironic aftermath, although divestment became standard for universities, it appeared to have no effect on South African policy.)

But of course most of all, OSU's faculty liked the possibility that Ed Jennings might bestir this university that's often tagged "a sleeping giant." They liked the idea that at last, Ohio State would get a little respect, a little class, that at last it would be in the academic big leagues and everyone would know it. In spring 1987, the Ohio State chapter of the American Association of University Professors gave Jennings its Louis Nemzer Award, which annually cites an outstanding faculty member. It was an extraordinary honor for a president.

By 1987–1988, Jennings was in his seventh year as Ohio State's president. In that, he said, he was atypical, at least in the Big Ten, where he had the second-longest tenure. He has described what keeps him going: "The best part, the exciting part of this job is the diversity. In any one day I go from a power-play issue to the cancer center to freshman English." But perhaps the seven years are showing when he gets back to his office after the student breakfast, and, contemplating a full in-basket, says, "Mostly it's kind of boring." Anyway, he goes through the papers at a good clip: forty-five seconds to write a note, thirty to write a shorter note, twenty-five to initial, and fifteen to read and discard copies of letters staffers wrote. Every week, he gets five to six hundred pieces of mail.

Promptly at ten o'clock there is a meeting in his office. The Kettering Foundation of Dayton is weighing sponsorship of an OSU program to increase affirmative-action awareness in university deans and vice-presidents. Now, in a meeting with Jennings, Provost Myles Brand, and three other university staffers, fund representative Estus Smith wants to see how committed Ohio State really is. In fact, affirmative action is one of Jennings's passions. The land-grant university was meant to provide access for minorities, he tells Smith, and it has to do so for blacks and Hispanics just as it did for Latvians, Poles, and Irish. If top administrators were more conscious of racism, they could help make the campus atmosphere better for black students. Jennings does suggest a wording change to OSU associate provost Barbara Newman, who is planning the program: "If you tell a bunch of deans and vice-presidents that you've got a leadership program, they'll tell you to buzz off. They're not going to stand still for a touchy-feely program on race awareness."

"To some extent," Jennings observes after the meeting ends at eleven, "that was fundraising." He returns to his paper work. He goes through a folder of clippings on higher education; he makes a note of one ("There's a good article on numbers of high-school grads . . ."); he gets out his laptop computer ("Twenty years ago, I started as an academic computer whizz") to check his agenda; he returns a phone call. It is a moment of calm in a day in which he has yet to give two speeches, receive or hand out a dozen plaques, and have a medal-bearing ribbon hung around his neck.

Ed Jennings believes that public universities will become academically dominant in the next century. They alone will benefit from "economies of scale"—for only the big will be able to afford greatness. Only an almost-billion-dollar institution like Ohio State can propose to spend a hundred million dollars on the library, can afford a laser research lab or a supercomputer. Also, he says, "in virtually every field it's no longer just the lone scholar. Much teaching and research are interdisciplinary." A large university has the resources for interdisciplinary initiatives—in a field like biological sciences, for example. With its diverse student body, the public institution is in step with a nation that's becoming increasingly heterogeneous. And finally, "we are still affordable. Anybody can come here."

The job of Ohio State's president has certain seasonal rhythms, Jennings says. Summer is "operational"—fixing roads and sewers, making sure everything is "ready for sixty thousand students who are about to arrive." Fall is legislative and operational—plus enrollment statistics. Winter is quietest. And May—with both the budget and year-end ceremonies—is frantic.

Jennings has a large, wood-paneled office overlooking the Oval. He has the fine, traditional furniture of many modern executives: the desk; the large walnut table where in the morning he met with the Kettering Foundation; and, by a window, a cluster of upholstered seats where, after lunch on this May Wednesday, he meets with botany Professor Tod Stuessy, who wants to give Jennings a plaque designed for contributors to the Herbarium, a systematics collection of dried plant materials. Stuessy has been having trouble raising money for the Herbarium, a dilemma for which Jennings, while expressing admiration for the science of classification, offers no particular suggestions.

What they do discuss are buckeye trees. Stuessy, eager to "raise consciousness about botany," suggests a botanical buckeye grove on campus. "There are thirteen species of buckeye," he says. "We could probably grow ten. It'd be fascinating." Jennings observes that it would promote Ohio as well as botany, and they agree to look into it.

The presidents of Ohio State University survive, at least, as building names. The first president, Edward Orton (1873–81), was honored by Orton Hall, which houses geology, his subject, and which many would agree is the best old building on campus. William Oxley Thompson was president for so long

(1899–1925) that he got the library named for him. However, since the William Oxley Thompson Library is almost always called the Main Library, Thompson also got a large statue of himself outside at the head of the Oval. Some presidents did less well. James Canfield (1895–99) got merely a dormitory. Howard Landis Bevis (1940–56) and George Rightmire (1926–38) got undistinguished buildings on west campus. Novice Fawcett (1956–72) lucked out with a showcase—a hotel, alumni-house, and meeting-room complex (including the room where the Board of Trustees meets) grandly called the Fawcett Center for Tomorrow.

It has not always been easy to be an effective president of Ohio State. It was particularly difficult in the late nineteenth century when ex-President of the United States Rutherford B. Hayes was on the Board and, accustomed to running things, ran the university. As William A. Kinnison writes in his book *Building Sullivant's Pyramid,* Hayes "had the experience, the prestige, and, having retired from politics and public life, the leisure to devote to the Ohio State University and its problems." At least, during Hayes's *de facto* presidency, the legislature in 1891 began to give the university an annual levy, which it had not provided before. But it was not until the William Oxley Thompson presidency that, as historian James Pollard says, Ohio State finally "grew to true university status," which presumably is why Thompson's statue dominates the Oval.

By the time Harold Enarson became president in 1972, the pundits had it that Ohio State was the independent fiefdoms of agriculture, athletics, and medicine; the president got what was left. Jennings suggests that even if that was true in the seventies, it is less true today: "The best comparison now is a decentralized conglomerate." He does not aver, though some observers would, that he has been a relatively strong president, that the traditional rich and independent powerhouses of the university have simply had less independence. Agriculture has less autonomy than it did in the seventies; the hospitals do continue to have a separate, if interlapping board. Jennings does point out that, in the context of the institution, athletics is not the financial megawonder people suppose. "We're about to approach a billion-dollar budget," he says. "Athletics is seventeen million. A very tiny portion." Even so, after Earle Bruce was fired, there was some debate as to whether the administration was running athletics or vice versa.

To his argument that the twenty-first century will be the age of public universities, Jennings adds his angle on Ohio State's history. "Today for the first time," he says, "growth or decline isn't the dominant factor driving this institution." He traces historic cycles of growth (the 1920s; after World War II) and decline (the Depression; wartime), followed by "consolidation" in the 1970s. "This is the first time in our history that we can concentrate our resources on the *quality* of the institution. Instead of roads we can build a special chemistry building; instead of a hospital, a cancer-research facility. If we do our job right now, we can emerge as a preeminent institution." Not only is excellence the destiny of Ohio State, but its destiny begins now.

So Jennings hopes. But he has been lucky to be at the helm in the eighties, when Ohio's governor and legislature were happy to support higher education in hopes of bolstering the economy. Though OSU has been more aggressive in soliciting private contributions in recent years, the state remains far and away the university's biggest single benefactor; and if there's one constant in the history of Ohio funding for higher education, it's capriciousness. Moreover, the state has never been wildly generous. In 1986–87 it lagged in the bottom ten states in appropriations per capita and per thousand dollars of personal income.

*　　*　　*

At 5 P.M. on Wednesday, May 11, Jennings shows up at the Ohio Union with a speech in each breast pocket. First he heads to a second-floor lounge for the annual meeting of Phi Beta Delta, an international honor society. During the opening remarks, Jennings sits in a front-row seat and reviews his speech. He says that every summer, he writes a very long speech, part of which he gives to the university senate in the fall and the rest of which provides a whole year's worth of verbiage.

When Jennings travels he often asks to meet local alumni ("They're part of Ohio State"); he has done so in places like Paris, Genoa, and Madrid. Now he tells the internationally-oriented Phi Beta Delta chapter about "one of the highlights of my visit to Beijing" in 1983: a meeting with eleven alumni—men and women who graduated from Ohio State in the early fifties. Studying at OSU when Mao came to power, they were offered political asylum by the U.S. but chose to return to mainland China. "These were people who had not just a thirty-year absence, but thirty years with no contact," Jennings says. "They wanted to know about buildings long gone—like the Armory." Later Jennings gets a Phi Beta Delta certificate and a medal on a red-and-gold ribbon. Afterward at the reception, a physics professor snags him to come meet his wife; he talks to a dentist, a historian, the men's tennis coach and two players (they're at an international confab because they play abroad; at least, in the Caribbean).

The president of the university tends its reputation. This is critical, because reputations, though they are themselves ephemeral, bring real rewards—talent, students, and money. When Jennings says Ohio State is "less than the sum of its parts," he is also saying that this institution may be undervalued, but only by mistake. He elaborates: "Our average academic department has a better reputation than the university as a whole. Our best departments have been in disciplines that have rarely attracted national attention. We haven't done the big medicine, the constitutional law, the big sexy stuff. I think it's happening. It's one reason we can hire six or seven prominent faculty every year."

Surprisingly little has been done to quantify American university reputations through in-depth surveys that will balance "the big sexy stuff" with insightful research and quality teaching. A Californian, Jack Gourman, puts out *The Gourman Reports,* which rank graduate and undergraduate programs at many U.S. institutions; his 1985 reports ranked Ohio State twenty-eighth overall of the top fifty graduate schools, thirty-third overall among the top undergraduate schools. But Gourman says his sources are "individuals who must remain anonymous," though he avers that they include university faculty, presidents, administrators, and trustees. Many in higher education find that too mysterious.

There are other appraisals, such as periodic assessments of certain graduate programs by the Conference Board of Associated Research Councils or comparisons of, say, business schools. Through 1987, *U.S. News & World Report* published annual rankings based on polls of presidents. (Ohio State, as we've seen, could have been more pleased with the 1987 results, which mentioned only OSU engineering.) Faced with charges of superficiality, *U.S. News* announced in June, 1988, that it would expand its survey.

One of the college guides, *Barron's Profiles of American Colleges,* lists institutions by how competitive their admissions are: They're ranked "most," "highly," "very," "competitive," "less," and "non." So long as it had open admissions, Ohio State was "noncompetitive"; after 1987, when it initiated selective admissions, the university was listed as "competitive." That dismayed OSU officials, who hoped for a "very" but, Jennings said, missed it by one point in the median ACT score of entering freshmen.

Jennings says he is not among those university presidents who have promised that their institution will be, say, one of the nation's five best in ten years: "I don't know how I could define that. Top five of what? Really, there are thirty or forty great American universities. Ohio State is one of them. There are an awful lot of myths about comparing universities.

"That doesn't mean you can't be ambitious."

When Ed Jennings leaves the Phi Beta Delta reception, he heads down the Ohio Union stairs to the ballroom, where at six o'clock the President's Undergraduate Leadership Awards dinner begins. He pauses en route to hand a staffer the plaque and medal he picked up at the last meeting; he wants his hands free.

The dinner brings together four hundred students, parents, faculty, and staff, who sit at long rows of round tables adorned with white cloths and red napkins. Before the meal begins, the diners hear Ed Jennings give what few of them realize is his second speech in an hour. Richard Hollingsworth, an assistant dean and affable emcee, follows. "You," he says to the students, "represent the best in leadership Ohio State has to offer." Senior Annabell Droz-Berrios appears on the platform to give an invocation, and the meal begins. The leaders, their admirers, and Ed Jennings, who began this day upstairs with yogurt, have miniature vegetables, spinach pasta, and coated boneless chicken breast for dinner.

Annabell Droz-Berrios has returned to her seat, where she picks at her food. She says she is a senior from Puerto Rico, a communications major who will soon graduate with the promise of a job at Procter and Gamble in Cincinnati. Tonight, she says, the ten outstanding seniors will be named. "So for some

it will be a very happy moment. For some, less so. I'm hoping
that when we don't make it we feel happy for those who do."
Droz-Berrios herself is a candidate for this award. Thinking
about it erodes her normal ebullience, and she is subdued,
even somber. "In 1985," she says, "I decided to leave my all-
Hispanic organizations on campus and join historically white
organizations. I wanted to expose middle-class Americans to
something different from what they expected. People think I
live in a shack in Puerto Rico. They think I carry knives.
Then later they say, 'You're so different from all the Puerto
Ricans I've met.' But that's just it. I'm not different." She
decides to try a bite of her chicken.

After dinner the members of the honorary societies, including Mortar Board and Sphinx (of which Annabell Droz-
Berrios is a member) appear on stage. Then thirty-five
undergraduates, including Kim Fullman of Students for Peace
and Justice, are cited for special accomplishments. The outstanding senior awards, the most prestigious, are last; they are
presented by President Jennings himself and Dan Heinlen of
the Alumni Association. Jennings is saying, "We have cap-
tains, presidents, kings, and queens—it's difficult to define an
outstanding senior." He adds that this group has a combined
grade-point average of 3.7.

The very first person to be named is Annabell Droz-Berrios, who gets a hug and a plaque from Ed Jennings and then
stands in the spotlight, looking anxious, even unhappy. Which
is how people look when they are trying not to cry.

Altogether Jennings hands out plaques to four men and six
women, and then leaves the platform before the anthem
"Carmen Ohio" begins. When at 9:10 the assembly in the
darkened ballroom comes to the last line ("How firm thy
friendship, O-hi-o"), he has slipped out into the night to find
his car. It has, after all, been a long day.

JUNE CALENDAR

Board Newcomer. A new trustee was at the board meeting June 3: Leslie Wexner, whose $25 million gift for the Wexner Center for the Visual Arts made him Ohio State's largest donor ever. To the board, he brought a businessman's point of view. First he suggested improved accounting for health claims. Then, after hearing that Ohio State's tuition was fifth of the Big Ten's nine public institutions, he asked why the price was so low: "If Ohio State were the most expensive, why would that be bad?" Two trustees and two administrators hastened to tell Wexner about the importance of accessibility, diversity, and the land-grant mission. "Ten years ago," Jennings said, "we were third in the Big Ten to Michigan and Michigan State, and we have purposely driven that down."

The trustees approved a salary hike for Jennings, whose income would rise 8 percent ($10,320) to $139,320. Big Ten presidents' salaries reportedly ranged from a low of $108,000 at Wisconsin to a high of $155,000 at Purdue. However, since the average OSU instructor's salary was $24,600 and the average professor's, $57,900, President Jennings's raise was widely criticized on campus, often in jokey asides.

News Item. In early June in New York, Rick Bay resigned his job with the Yankees and took one with a television group.

Evacuation. After final exams ended June 9, the Lincoln Tower parking lot was filled with cars removing jean jackets, typewriters, plastic milk crates, book bags, board games (Risk), suitcases, shirts on hangers, and black plastic bags stuffed with laundry to other locations, such as Richland County, Ohio.

Spring Commencement. Spring commencement, the only one of the year held outdoors in Ohio Stadium, started at 9:30 Friday morning, June 10; 5,420 degrees were conferred. The graduates, divided by college, sat in the curve of the horseshoe; their friends and families watched from the sides. On the field were band and speakers' platforms, plus some fifty tables holding diplomas.

Tom Spring, a University Communications staffer who sat with the press, brought his daughter Erin, four, to see her mother, Rita, get an M.A. Erin, though dressed up for the occasion in a pink coat, was not impressed ("I hate this, Daddy."). However, for most people, thousands of exhilarated graduates in black robes by themselves made an occasion. This one was ornamented by honorary degrees to artist Roy Lichtenstein, architect Philip Johnson, and the head of the National Science Foundation, Erich Bloch, who was commencement speaker.

Handing out diplomas took more than an hour; it was almost noon when the last one went to Teri Perkins Zeise of Columbus, for a B.A. in social work. By then almost everyone had left. The deserted seats in the horseshoe curve were strewn with debris—programs, confetti, empty champagne bottles.

Pitcher Jennings. During the weekend, 2,800 OSU employees and guests relaxed at a Columbus Clippers baseball game. A pregame tailgate party featured mascot Brutus Buckeye and the music faculty band, the High Street stompers. Ed Jennings threw the first pitch.

Deconstructivist Construction. On June 12, the Wexner Center for the Visual Arts became the country's prime example of Deconstructivist architecture. It was so anointed in *The New York Times Magazine* by design critic Joseph Giovannini, who characterized the OSU campus as "the most traditional of campuses in the most American of cities" and then promised the Wexner Center would be "one of the most unsettling structures in the United States. The path through the building is a stroll into uncertainty."

Deconstructivism was a concept hatched that summer by a Museum of Modern Art show in New York, but the forty-three-million-dollar Wexner Center had been around for years—ever since its architects, New York's Peter Eisenman and Columbus's Richard Trott, an OSU alumnus, won the arts center design contest in 1983. Construction, begun in 1985, was still underway: In June the building looked like a tall, asymmetrical jungle gym at the foot of the Oval. Yet to emerge were brick tower segments designed to echo the castle-like Armory on this site before 1958.

Nationally, Deconstructivism generated an architectural furor. This was largely ignored in Columbus, except at the School of Architecture, where Assistant Professor Jeffrey Kipnis said it was not unusual for the term to come after the design—that happened also with Pop Art. "The term is useful in giving us a way to break into new art," he said. "Basically, Deconstructivism tries to disturb by moving from within." To do that, it brings out repressed design elements, such as the asymmetry repressed in symmetry or the fragmentation repressed in the wholeness of a column—thus, the pieces of Armory tower. Donor Les Wexner was pleased: "I look forward with great anticipation to this world-class building."

Freshman Integration. The June 20 start of summer quarter saw virtually all freshman classes back on main campus after many years of isolation on west campus. In 1965, when Ohio State was expected to reach an enrollment of 75,000, thirteen buildings were planned for an in-house, twelve-thousand-student community college on west campus. Then in the early 1970s, after schools like Wright State, Akron, and Youngstown State came into the state university system, the legislature put a limit on OSU's enrollment. Ohio State halted further construction and used the five buildings it already had for freshman classes, a plan that freshmen never did like.

Summer Roamers. Summer-quarter enrollment in Columbus was down to 20,000, compared to 53,000 the autumn before. But 423 faculty were thus free to go abroad on lecture or study tours. They headed for sixty-four countries; the most popular destination was England.

7,397 Welcomes. Regular orientation programs for students entering fall quarter began June 21. Altogether, by September 21, 7,397 freshmen would attend twenty-six orientation programs.

Scrubbed: The Mirror Lake Scrub. And on June 25, because of the water crisis, the crews of Charles Smith, roads and grounds superintendent, did *not* open the Mirror Lake drain so as to give the pond's brick-lined basin its annual cleaning. It was the driest June ever and water use was restricted. Thus the bottles, coins, bicycles, four-hundred-pound aggregate trash cans, and smelly silt that Smith knew he would find at the bottom of Mirror Lake waited to be cleared out in another year. For sure, it would be in summer, because it was easier to do the job with fewer people around. Said Smith, "Students see fish down in the muck and try to save them."

CHAPTER 10

Buckeye-ism

At half time during the November 14 Iowa game—the game which ended as Earle Bruce's third consecutive and last loss for Ohio State—an official ceremony took place on the fifty-yard line. On the very numerals 5 and 0, President Jennings stood with an easel and two botany professors, Tod Stuessy and the department chairman, Dan Crawford. The easel held a large, ornate, gilded frame, which displayed a twig.

With its wizened yellow-green leaves and brown flowers, the twig was no ordinary piece of tree. It was, to botanists, the original buckeye. It was the type specimen—the very one that German botanist Carl Ludwig Willdenow was looking at when he described the species, *Aesculus glabra,* in 1809. Now on loan from the Berlin Botanical Garden, it had come to spend two and a half years at Ohio State. This ceremony in Ohio Stadium was called, "The Buckeye Has Come Home!!"

For two minutes, while Kevin Fitzsimons took fourteen black-and-white pictures of the three men and the easel, the voice on the public address system explained the significance of the twig. Then Stuessy and Crawford took the buckeye up to the goalpost for more pictures with costumed mascot Brutus Buckeye and two cheerleaders. With that, the original buckeye had officially arrived.

The Ohio buckeye is a tree whose name has somehow become a nickname for people from Ohio, for people from Ohio State, and particularly, for OSU athletes. Tod Stuessy was especially interested in all this. "It is kind of strange for a university to have a plant for a mascot," he explained. "Indiana State are the sycamores. Two community colleges—one in Scottsdale and one in Hawaii—have plants. That's all. It's special—it's an opportunity for botany to get a little recognition."

The buckeye, really, is not much of a tree. It's related to the horse chestnut and it does grow in Ohio, though for many years the largest specimen has been in Kentucky. The tree's main virtue is probably its mahogany-colored seed, the size of an olive, decorated with a tan circle and said to resemble the eye of a deer. The seed is not edible, but it is decorative. The tree, however, is neither easy to grow nor decorative once grown. The seeds need a year or two in the ground before they will sprout and then, says campus horticulturist John Nagy, "They get leaf scorch real bad and look like they're dying all the time."

Not only is the buckeye a lousy tree, but the original Ohio buckeye probably was not from Ohio. Willdenow grew it in the Berlin Botanical Garden, where he planted a seed someone sent him from North America. Who sent it and, even more significantly, where he found it, are unknown. Stuessy says it probably came from some other state. Then, stretching for *some* connection, he suggests it must have been collected around the time Ohio became a state in 1803. Fortunately, as myth and mascot, the Ohio buckeye has long since moved beyond any real need for facts.

It was audacious of Stuessy to ask the Berlin Botanical Garden for the original buckeye. He began in 1985, when, in his capacity as director of the Ohio State Herbarium, he wrote to Berlin and offered to buy the buckeye. He said he would pay ten thousand dollars. He didn't have ten thousand dollars, but in the unlikely event the Germans said yes, he figured he could get it. Failing purchase, he offered to trade for it or borrow it. After two years of his entreaties, the Germans agreed to a loan, beginning in summer 1987. "It was a special concession," Stuessy says. "They have a policy of never loaning anything."

In spring 1988, Stuessy took the original buckeye on tour. People at Ohio State alumni clubs in Greenville, Wooster, and Salina could gape through the Plexiglas at the long-dead twig in the gold frame. For traveling, Stuessy put the frame in a rigid, foam-lined protective case he'd had made: It looked like an oversized suitcase, was reinforced like a steamer trunk, and was just large enough that it took two people to carry it.

Stuessy had no doubt that going on the road was worthwhile. Even a lot of Ohioans wonder what, exactly, a buckeye is, so botanical distortions are common. For instance, people mistakenly call the buckeye seed a nut, which it is not even if it does look like one. Also, Stuessy has noticed that an OSU logo design represents "botanical impossibilities—naked seeds coming out from the leaf petiole. Not to know what a buckeye is makes us look foolish."

While Stuessy did his bit for botanical education, he pointed out that the football team contributes too. Since the days of Woody Hayes, he said, football players have been rewarded for big plays with "more of these compound palmate leaves on their helmet. A palmate leaf is shaped like the palm of your hand; the buckeye really has five leaflets making up one leaf. So every time ABC zeroes in on the huddle, there's a little botanical information for America." It is quintessential Ohio State: football, erudition, and buckeyes all at once.

School spirit is ardent loyalty to the institution. It is hard to quantify, but Ohio State has it. It is most conspicuous in football season, but its manifestations can show up anywhere—on the golf course, for instance, where three of the sandtraps spell out O S U. Or, in the rowboats at Stone Lab: All seventeen are painted gray and scarlet (the scarlet might, to an untutored eye, look like red but is no mere red in name). Even the campus bus routes are called Scarlet and Gray, though at least one driver laments that this system confuses riders. He wishes the route names would go back to North and South.

In ways both expected and unexpected, Ohio State saves itself or fragments of its past. Unexpectedly, it saves an empty water tower. On a grassy knoll on west campus, the 500,000-gallon water tower looms, its rounded gray sides emblazoned with the name of the university, in scarlet. From the nearby Route 315, it looks like an enormous sign; it has a landmark quality. That was probably why, when it was no longer needed to regulate pressure and went on the market late in 1986, it was snatched off the market before anyone could bid.

The university *is* expected to save its old papers, the records of its institutional history, though the ROTC building may be an improbable place to keep them. ("We've been here since 1980," says Raimund Goerler, who heads University Archives, "and to this day they insist there's no room for us.") Goerler, who came to OSU in 1978, says there is "a common supposition that the institutional archivist contains the institutional memory between his ears"—a supposition he denies even as he spouts quirky facts about Ohio State history. For instance, a trustee who was once an OSU cheerleader, Herb Atkinson, willed that his ashes be stored in the wall of Bricker Hall, where they are. Or, only one faculty member has been executed for murder: James Snook, who taught veterinary medicine, in 1929 shot a student he'd been having an affair with. "Chloroform in print" is how Goerler characterizes the official university histories, except for the first volume and the latest, Paul Underwood's *The Enarson Years.*

Bertha Ihnat, who in 1960 came to OSU as a student because she liked the band, now presides over the Archives' reference room, where an elderly widower searched yearbooks to find the name of a woman he dated in the thirties. (Then he dashed off to the alumni office to get her address and the Archives never did get a follow-up.) Bulletins from 1922–23 reveal that students were taking courses in "Primitive Man in Ohio" and "Railway Engineering." A notebook holds a study of Ohio State people in the 1946 *Who's Who:* of 40,145 people listed, 518, or 1.29 percent, went to OSU. And the most frequently consulted work of all in Archives is John Herrick's *Campus Buildings.*

Archives has football programs but no papers from its second president, Walter Q. Scott, who held the office only two years, which may not have been time enough for papers too. It does have student astronomy papers from 1917, and a rope rug and scrap book that belonged to Admiral Richard Byrd, the polar explorer. OSU artifacts are few. They include a bowler hat said to have belonged to President William Oxley Thompson and roof tiles from Orton Hall. Archives also has 650,000 photos, which Goerler calls "an unusually large collection. We were the second public university to begin teaching photography."

It is up to Goerler to see that Archives gets the stuff it should have. He has the Printing Facility save a copy of everything, which he culls (he doesn't want blank forms). Through this arrangement, Archives, which is the ultimate repository, sometimes has material before anyone else. Goerler wants material from two hundred campus departments or offices but not from campus mail or the laundry. Once he visited the laundry, which had called to see if it should save its financial and statistical papers. He didn't think much of the records but was impressed by the laundering, particularly the machines that fold sheets.

The archives are not all that Ohio State saves of its past. There are also the old University Hall, films, and Novice Fawcett, who was president before last.

University Hall, which was not quite finished when school opened September 17, 1873, was the first building of The Ohio State University. It was an all-purpose building, for classes and living and, ultimately, weddings, commencements, and protest meetings. University Hall stood for Ohio State so completely that when it was torn down in 1971, it was re-placed with a similar-looking structure.

And in fact, the old University Hall was torn down and then kept. The new building memorializes the old one not only in appearance but also by reusing a few of its bricks and window frames. And at two sites that are off but near cam-pus, OSU saves other pieces of the old building. Some are at a fenced masonry storeyard, where bricks made on the origi-nal construction site rest on rotting wooden pallets.

The others are in the classroom furniture pool warehouse, which is managed by Bill Condon. As buildings are remodeled (in 1987–88, Lazenby Hall), the furniture—even the black-boards—is stored here temporarily. But the floor registers, stamped-metal ceiling tiles, leaded-glass windows, eight-foot doors, and doorframes for eighteen-inch walls—these relics of the old University Hall seem destined to remain forever. A dark wooden newell post is the size of a lectern; the solid black walnut railing is smooth from a century of hands. A piece of the railing is missing, Condon says. It was used to make a gavel that President Fawcett presented to President Nixon.

Tom Snider oversees the Photography and Cinema Depart-ment's film archives, which holds three million feet of movies made at and of Ohio State. That's enough for almost two months' worth of round-the-clock viewing, which would include the blimp landing on the Oval in the 1920s; an English faculty lunch in 1957; 1934 student life and faculty golf in 1930; a 1964 movie of the 1939 class reunion; a student film on slums ("Columbus: All America City"); Carl Reiner, Henry Winkler, and Gerald Ford visiting campus; and football games continuously from 1930 on.

The football films were useful for putting together a video on the 1954 season, with Woody Hayes doing the narration. It was released in the fall of 1987 and within eight months seven hundred sold at $29.95. The proceeds support a scholarship, Snider says. In the summer of 1988 he was working on a sequel: the 1968 season. Those were the two perfect seasons—1954 and 1968—when OSU won the Big Ten, the Rose Bowl, and the national championship.

And do the film archives get a lot of calls from people who want to see the 1952 Purdue game or faculty golf in 1930? "Well, no," Snider says. "No one knows I've got this."

And hardly anyone knows that Novice G. Fawcett, president of Ohio State from 1956 to September 2, 1972, is still on campus. It has been a couple of years since he went to the Faculty Club. "You see," he explains, "when you've been away from an institution as long as I have, they're mostly strangers." Fawcett keeps office hours two or three days a week. In summer 1988, he is seventy-nine, which has diminished his agility but not his resonant voice, his stature—he is six feet four—or his large, purposeful hands. He has an office in the Fawcett Center for Tomorrow, the hotel, meeting-room, and alumni complex that, he says, he worked twelve years to raise the money for—"It was built without state funds except for the land"—though he didn't *expect* it to be named for him. When it was, and when he saw the sign with his name, he was startled. It seemed just like a tombstone.

Novice Fawcett, who is often recalled as OSU's "last presi-

dent who didn't have a doctorate" (he says he had much of
the work on one finished at OSU; he is still sore that resi-
dency requirements were changed after he had enrolled),
came to the university presidency from a post as superintendent of Columbus schools. "That was a very unusual move,"
he says. "Very few presidents of comprehensive universities
have come from public school administration. As a matter of
fact I don't know of any, except one on a small scale—he was
president of the University of Wyoming."

The sixteen years of Fawcett's presidency saw a doubling of
OSU's enrollment, from 22,500 to 46,000. "During my tenure
we built about a hundred buildings," he says. "As I recall,
they cost between three- and four-hundred-million dollars." It
was also a tumultuous time on campus, with student unrest,
the arrival of the National Guard, and the closing of the university May 6–19, 1970. "I went through a lot of controversy
during my years," Fawcett says. "I've always had a feeling
those tragic shootings at Kent State marked the beginning of
the end of that sort of thing in this country. I've thought
about this a great deal."

Since his retirement Fawcett has been on the boards of cor-
porations and of a traffic safety foundation; he has been on an
OSU fund-raising committee and has helped pick eminent
scholars for faculty appointments. "I still even get requests to
write recommendations," he says. "When people find out
you're alive, they ask you to do all manner of things."

In 1987–88, people bought about nineteen-million-dollars'-
worth of Ohio State sweatshirts, gift-wrap bows that play the
fight song, and other paraphernalia. In fact, in Columbus ten
retailers were selling only OSU merchandise. All of it—every
last OSU pillow or sock or ear muff or suspenders—brought
income to the university: over $600,000 in fiscal 1988.

Actually, selling the right to use OSU logos started in 1974, not long after a university vice-president was appalled to see the official seal on toilet seats. Starting that year, the name, the seal, the logos, and expressions like Go Bucks were registered as trademarks, and manufacturers were expected to send in royalties. Often, they didn't bother. Then in the early eighties, a staffer named Anne Chasser noticed that a licensee was behind in payments. She called, and when the next day the company sales manager flew in from New York to deliver a fourteen-thousand-dollar check, she realized licensing might have the charm of found money. Chasser organized an effective program, with the virtues of low overhead and high income.

The income goes into a scholarship fund ("The fastest-growing scholarship fund," Chasser says) that has $1.2 million and disbursed $40,460 to forty-nine students in the fall of 1987. The 445 licensees were producing everything for a head-to-toe, wall-to-wall, morning-to-night, home-to-office, mealtime-to-playtime OSU environment. Even toilet seats, though none with the official seal. Chasser says Ohio State won't license anything junky or in bad taste, and she does the judging. She holds up a red plastic mug with a gray OSU logo on the side. "I personally would never buy this, but there's a market for it." Though she's dressed in OSU colors—a gray plaid suit and red blouse—Chasser herself is a University of Dayton graduate. She majored in American studies, which she finds appropriate now: "This is a slice of Americana, isn't it?"

Some people express their affection for OSU by giving something to the university. In fact, OSU has sixty-five development officers, one of whom, Michael Fellows, is in charge of gifts of property. "We tend," says Fellows, "to look for gifts in harmony with our academic mission. It's important for us to remember this is not just a repository for gifts." The university solicits some academically useful gifts, like the skulls the dental school was looking for or the potato-chip machine in food sciences.

People give real estate to Ohio State: Two retired school teachers donated 12.88 acres of Palmdale, California. Sometimes people *try* to give real estate to the university, but the university won't accept it. For example, Fellows, who is on the road every month to look at property, looked at some in northern Michigan on a day when the water was high. "I stood in ankle-deep water and in four directions, there was no land."

Fellows has been on the job five years. Once when he first started, he opened a box and found a coffee can filled with an alumnus's ashes. "It wasn't so much a gift," says Fellows. "He just wanted someone to put them under a tree on campus—he left money for the tree." Well, Fellows did as the man wished, but he hastens to add, "That's not something the university ordinarily does."

Devoted alumni are no exception for Ohio State but they do flourish, especially in Bryan, Ohio, a place where allegiance to Ohio State is so significant that sometimes it's claimed by people who went to other colleges. This may be because Bryan is on the defensive geographically. The town, which has a population of eight thousand and is where Dum-Dum lollipops and Etch-A-Sketch toys are made, is the seat of Wood County, at the northwest corner of Ohio. Indiana is to the west, Michigan to the north, and both East Lansing and Ann Arbor are closer than Columbus.

Of devoted alumni, dentists are especially devoted, though even for a dentist, Norman Burns is extreme. He says, "Many years ago, Woody Hayes said, 'Give me the name of an OSU dentist in a community, and I've got somebody who's going to help me.'" Hayes never had a problem with support in Bryan, where Burns, a 1957 graduate of the College of Dentistry, lives and practices. Burns went to the University of Toledo for his undergraduate work; he has always felt a little guilty that he didn't have the same enthusiasm for Toledo that he had for

OSU. What he most values about Toledo, though, is the bachelor's degree that led him to Ohio State.

Norman Burns has been such a passionate Ohio State alumnus, has been so partisan, has bought everything, joined everything, and flies the flag, that it is hard to believe he doesn't fit the stereotype of an oversized, overloud Joe-College-Forever type. He is in fact compact and wiry; he has a shock of straight gray hair; he speaks quietly. But he has poured so much energy into being an Ohio State alumnus, that it has been virtually a second career for him. "Half a lifetime," he says.

Here's what he's done as an alumnus. He's been active in clubs. He was a president of the OSU dental alumni. And in 1960 he was a cofounder of the Williams County alumni club, which has met annually in the spring ever since. Burns has attended every time except once, when he was sick in the late sixties. He says the meetings have never drawn fewer than ninety-four people (that was 1986, when an academician spoke) and have had as many as 229 (in 1974, when Woody Hayes was speaker). "Athletics draws people," Burns says. "The world's number one physicist wouldn't."

He's been an Ohio State resource for Bryan. When people there want something that has to do with Ohio State, they turn to Norm Burns. That's how the high school got Woody Hayes as commencement speaker in 1979. The speech—complete with Hayes phrases like, "You don't pay back. You pay forward"—was "elegant," Burns says. "We played it on the radio the day he died."

He's covered Ohio State football as a photographer for the Bryan *Times*. That started in 1977, when the editor needed someone to take pictures because his son, who had been doing it, had graduated from medical school. The editor coaxed Burns into it, even though Burns knew nothing about photography—which is why at first he would set off with the newspaper's camera preset and preloaded. But he found he liked the perks on this job: "I have press credentials. I have the same courtesies as a writer from *The Toledo Blade* or *Sports Illustrated*. They allow me into the Press Box for pregame charbroiled steak, onto the sidelines, and into the locker room after the game." So Burns became a skilled photographer. He now owns two cameras and has his own darkroom.

He promoted Ohio State at home. Burns's wife, Donna, an artist, is an Ohio State graduate. All three of their children earned Ohio State degrees. The youngest, Martha Jo, "iced the cake for us," as her father says, and became an OSU cheerleader in 1984. In the summer of 1988 she was living in Columbus and engaged to a founder of the local Young Bucks Club.

He has acquired the symbols. In his yard, Norm Burns has three young buckeye trees. Being genuine, they "look like they're dying," as campus horticulturist Nagy would say. An OSU banner is on the flagpole. The van in the driveway is scarlet and gray. Donna Burns painted on the block O and buckeye leaves; the horn plays the Ohio State fight song; the interior is scarlet and gray, with GO BUCKS pillows. A veteran of ninety thousand miles in trips to Columbus, the van now goes only to the local airport to pick up OSU club speakers. (Besides the ride, the speakers all get Dum-Dums and Etch-A-Sketches.)

He has two roomfuls of memorabilia. Burns's house has a Buckeye Room and a Buckeye Basement, which are scarcely enough to hold all the mementos—such as the pictures of Burns with OSU coaches and presidents. Donna would like him to clean up all the stuff, but after all, it's half a lifetime. He says, "I don't know of any institution in the state that touches more people that Ohio State."

But it does touch some more than others.

JULY CALENDAR

Fallen Landmark. The Logan Elm, a victim of Dutch elm disease, was cut down early in July. "We really felt badly about that," horticulturist John Nagy said. The tree had been slow to leaf out in the spring; by the end of June, it was completely brown. At least, in the springs of eighty-seven and eighty-eight, Nagy had collected sixty seeds directly from its branches. He hoped to plant new Logan Elms all over campus.

Drought 1988. The Logan Elm wasn't all Nagy had to worry about, for that July there was dead Kentucky bluegrass all over campus. Dry weather, aggravated by the hottest summer since the 1950s, had brought a severe drought to the Midwest, the state, and the OSU campus; grass and crops were dying; and water use was restricted—on July 5 the university even shut off the sprinklers at President Jennings's house and the Faculty Club.

For coping with the heat, Forrest Smith, a physician with University Health Service, recommended cool clothing, water drinking, and air-conditioning. He said he had treated some students for heat exhaustion; they'd been working outdoors, experienced nausea and dizziness.

The weather was giving OSU its highest electric bill ever— over one million dollars just for the month of July. Shepherd

Ron Guenther also had record bills. On Monday, July 18 he bought fifty tons of New York State hay at $185 a ton; normally, he paid seventy dollars a ton. "No hay's available in Ohio," he said. "Oh, there's some, but everybody's locked their doors, waiting for the price to go out of sight." However, his sheep each eat five pounds of hay a day. "We had our backs to the wall."

Later that same day, half an inch of rain fell during the evening rush hour: the beginning of the end of the drought. By July 25, a week later, seven inches of rain had fallen. People started to call Ron Guenther to see if he still needed hay. The price dropped to $160 a ton.

Evolution at the Holiday Inn. In mid-July, eleven biologists and eleven philosophers came from all parts of the United States, from Canada, and England to discuss evolution at the Holiday Inn on Lane, across the street from OSU. For five days, they met at a round table in the hotel's Buckeye Suite and talked while fifteen to twenty observers, mostly from OSU and Kenyon College, watched. Among the biologists was Stephen Jay Gould of Harvard University; among the philosophers was Sandra Mitchell, who represented Ohio State. Mitchell is a philosopher of science—she studies knowledge by looking at science, where "our knowledge is more secure" than it is in art, for example.

At the evolution conference, the questions included these: Is evolution different in sexual and asexual organisms? Does evolution proceed gradually or in spurts? What does "fittest"—as in "survival of the fittest"—mean? Afterward, Sandra Mitchell summed up: "Before the middle of the nineteenth century, philosophy and biology were the same subject. At this conference, the division blurred. If you didn't know the players, you couldn't tell who was a philosopher and who was a biologist." That in itself was one of the insights to emerge.

Smart Politics? The next week in Atlanta the Democrats nominated Massachusetts Governor Michael Dukakis for president and Lloyd Bentsen, a senator from Texas, for vice-president. An inquiring camera from *The Lantern* asked six students to assess Dukakis's choice of Bentsen as his running mate. All six thought it was smart politics, though Herb Gillen, a junior majoring in political science, pointed out that Bush would probably carry Texas anyway.

Police Reports. On July 14 a shoplifter stole four hundred dollars' worth of jogging suits, boxer shorts, and T-shirts from Conrads College Gifts across the street from OSU. Campus auto thefts were way up in 1988—thirty cars had been stolen by the end of July, compared to ten in all of 1987. One car was counted two times in the 1988 statistics: A graduate student's Pontiac was taken twice from the same parking lot. The first time, it was recovered. And on July 22 police seized ten pounds of cocaine in a campus area apartment. OSU police reported eight on-campus drug offenses so far in 1988, compared to seven in all of 1987. Most were for marijuana.

Ticket Refunds. The Athletic Ticket office had to send football ticket refunds to eight hundred faculty and staff when requests went over the fifteen-thousand-seat allotment. Faculty and staff priorities in tickets were based on a point system, which assigned more points to higher ranks and higher salaries.

CHAPTER 11

Is "Learning as Related to Agriculture" Still Relevant?

Ohio State University has the biggest working farm in the middle of a large city, anywhere. Because they're in a city, the farm's nine hundred acres are worth almost eighty million dollars; probably, this is the most valuable farm, anywhere. Here an acre that could sell for $85,000 produces a corn crop worth $240. Cattle ruminate in pastures where offices with mauve reception areas would, if they could, sprout with the abandon of dandelions. In an age when the bottom line is so highly esteemed, the farm has a giddy absurdity.

The farm represents traditional agriculture, perhaps even, from OSU's point of view, an obsolescent agriculture. That's a concern of Craig Fendrick, who manages crops for university farms. "The College of Agriculture," he says, "has become more oriented toward teaching individuals who provide assistance to agriculture rather than production agriculture. We hear bio this and bio that. You can still be taught production agriculture, but we're moving away from that. This university was founded as Ohio Agricultural and Mechanical. I think it's forgotten its roots as a land-grant university."

In the 1980s, few segments of the university faced so much change—and so much uncertainty—as the College of Agriculture. Enrollments plummeted, a quarter of the faculty retired, and high tech arrived: Newcomers like gene splicing and cell studies invaded agricultural labs.

The farms have always been part of the university. Of course, they were not planned to be in the city; the city just kept arriving. By 1987–88 Columbus and suburban Upper Arlington had long since surrounded west campus, where the university kept its poultry (five thousand to eight thousand chickens) and, with 210 acres of supporting crop and pasture, its dairy (110 cows in milk). Years before, in 1971, most of the livestock operations—beef, swine, horses, Ron Guenther's sheep—had relocated eight miles north in the rural environs of Don Scott Field, the OSU airport. But in 1971 no one knew that in that part of Columbus, land values were going to jump thirty times in ten years; by the eighties, the area would be one of the fastest-growing in the state. By then traffic would be so heavy that OSU could move its farm machinery during rush hours without holding anybody up.

The farms and the adjacent fields used for plant studies have a purpose for Ohio State: teaching and research. The university reasons that, to be used, facilities should be close. A cow can go to class in Plumb Hall. A graduate student can bicycle to his research plot. Bill Pope, an animal science professor in reproduction research, can plan an experiment that calls for working with pigs every four hours. When Kentucky moved its farm operations out of Lexington, or Nebraska moved its out of Lincoln, "use decreased tremendously," according to Craig Fendrick.

However, an OSU animal takes more than stall space. It also has supporting pasture and cropland nearby. The cropland produces corn and alfalfa for silage—roughage the animal needs. Paradoxically, this silage grown on expensive urban real estate is the cheap feed, with direct costs of twenty-two dollars a ton. A cow could eat bagged feed instead, Fendrick says. That would cost $225 a ton and be equivalent to living on T-bone steak—costly and not the best diet. Or, Fendrick could raise the five thousand tons of silage at OSU's rural Molly Caren Agricultural Center west of Columbus near London. He had 650 acres in grain there—corn and soybeans he would sell to support silage production in town. But he could put in silage instead and haul five hundred semi loads to town for fifty to sixty dollars a ton. It would still be absurdly expensive. In-town animals mandated in-town crops.

The OSU farms are real farms, but with differences. For instance, seen from the road, the dairy complex is a cluster of silos, an old-fashioned red barn, trees, even—sometimes—laundry on the line. But this is a picturesque family farm without a house; Kevin and Debbie Snyder have a two-room apartment in a corner of the main barn. Since 1984 he has been assistant herdsman. He met his wife, a dairy science major, when she was a student employee; by the summer of 1988 they have been in the apartment two years and both their children—one an infant son—were born here. Their daughter, Mary, two, already knows her dairy breeds, though she calls Guernseys "Gomer." The tricycle and the plastic pool in the yard are hers.

But at this dairy where all the cows have numbers in their ears (such as, 124J), parking is regulated (OSU DECALS ONLY). Visitors come all the time: two busloads of children a day in spring, fifty walk-ins a week all year, people who drive in to see the cows at eleven at night. Once Kevin Snyder got so he could sleep through the student employees' arriving for the 5 A.M. milking, he liked living at the dairy except for one thing. "Some days it's kind of depressing because I never leave." In the middle of Columbus, he was stuck on the farm.

Animals raised at OSU must meet its particular needs—for steak, for instance; the joke has it that the good beef goes to the Faculty Club and the rest to dining halls. Animals live, die, and breed by the OSU calendar. Take broiler chickens. Their whole egg-to-table life cycle runs ten weeks—just right for a quarter. Horses are bred for a class, Animal Science 581, equine reproductive management. First the mares are inseminated so that they'll foal for the beginning of spring quarter, in late March or early April. Stallions are subject to semen collections every class period.

Swine, ready to have their fat evaluated, show up for class on west campus. In turn, students travel north to see the swine in their home barn. Twenty at a time, the students tromp in to practice ear notching and tail docking, teeth cutting and castrating. Among the one thousand animals he manages, Swineherd Gary Stitzlein always has to have *bad* examples for teaching—such as stiff legs and small inside toes; he even has a few pigs *bred* to be fat. But he says research is really what makes this operation different from the average farm. "We spend more time weighing pigs, weighing feed, taking milk samples. Unless you've milked a sow you can't imagine what it's like to milk sixteen a day, each with fourteen nipples."

Other large agriculture schools, such as Cornell, Purdue, Michigan State, Iowa State, the University of California at Irvine, are in small towns or at the outskirts of their communities. That means they don't have neighbors who adore or deplore them for their rusticity—their romping lambs, their smelly manure. A city location also means development, which chops land up into small fields that are hard to farm. On west campus, Craig Fendrick's crews worked 140 acres in eight separate patches, one as small as ten acres. That made farming inefficient, because moving machinery is a slow business. To get a planter across a road to another field takes forty to sixty minutes: half to get ready, half to restart. "We spend twenty-five percent of our time moving," Fendrick says.

In spring 1988 OSU cultivated three hundred acres in Columbus—only half the acreage of just two years before. A cluster of brand-new buildings—such as the Woody Hayes Athletic Center, which took thirty-five acres—were sprouting in place of corn and alfalfa. So long as the livestock remain in Columbus, Fendrick said, the university agreed to leave a minimum of two hundred acres—one hundred at Don Scott, one hundred at west campus—for silage. Otherwise, he appreciated the university's other needs; he *expected* to lose land. (Less land wouldn't leave Fendrick without work; his mainstay was running OSU's Farm Science Review, which drew 115,000 agriculturists to the London farm every September.) OSU Campus Planner Jean Hansford affirmed that the farmland was available for other university purposes; indeed, planning maps show hundreds of acres as potential research parks. "Our campus," Hansford explained, "has flexibility." To Fendrick, though, it boiled down to the elemental question: "If you're not a production agriculture college, what facilities are necessary?" He paused and then added, "Fortunately, I don't have to make that decision."

The changes that beset the College of Agriculture in the 1980s were typical of those facing ag schools across the country. Certainly, OSU agriculture was basically secure: The 1862 Morrill Act, which established land-grant colleges, was clear in its mandate "to teach such branches of learning as are related to agriculture." But in the nineteenth century a big part of the population was on farms: 43.8 percent in 1880; by 1987, it was less than 2 percent. In Ohio in the 1980s alone, harvested acreage slumped 10 percent and the value of farmland plummeted by 45 percent. Everyone remembered pictures of heavily indebted rural families losing their farms.

One result was a 50 percent drop in ag students in ten

years. The College of Agriculture had 2,504 undergraduate majors in 1977, but it had only 1,255 in 1987. Losses were sharp in agricultural production: Agronomy (plant crops) was down two thirds; dairy science, a third; animal science, almost a third. The losses were steeper in the two areas that attracted urban students to the college in the 1970s: Horticulture was down 75 percent, and natural resources, almost two thirds.

When enrollment in the fall of 1987 slipped by only about 2 percent, Assistant Dean Harold Bauman called it a "plateau, which beats the hell out of the five to seven percent decline we've been running each year. Has the worm turned?" With his white hair and mustache, his six-foot stature, Bauman, an agricultural economist, was an impressive figure. Now, in the middle of June 1988, amid the harvest golds and greens of his office decor, he was saying that the farm crisis hurt enrollment, but in fact, "most of our students won't farm. Last Friday we graduated a hundred and fifty students, and less than a dozen will go back to the farm." Over the previous decade only 4 to 10 percent of graduates had gone into farming, though 40 percent went into agribusiness—machinery, feed, seed, and chemicals.

It was mainly urban students who were deserting the college. In the mid seventies 60 percent of OSU's students in agriculture came from urban backgrounds; in 1987, it was 20 percent. One reason for the drop in urban students was earlier overenthusiasm. In the seventies, as part of a back-to-the-soil movement, urban students thronged into horticulture. In due course, they glutted labor markets. Starting salaries were still low.

The School of Natural Resources also suffered in the job market, but a waning of environmentalism hurt even more. In fall 1987, the school had 242 students, way below the 1973 peak of 863. "Those kids were long on idealism," said John Disinger, acting director. "I would guess a lot of them felt they could change the world, but then all the rhetoric didn't translate into jobs. The kids now do well, but I'd like to think the kids that come through here are sharp kids that can move up the ladder. Last week a fellow walked in. He graduated in 1974. He did start in wildlife management and got a master's in landscape architecture at the University of Vermont. Now he's an investment broker."

Placement rates and salaries were good for food-science graduates, so to the College of Agriculture, food science began to look like a life saver. Vice-President Frederick Hutchinson observed that Ohio had a thousand food processors with twenty billion dollars in annual sales. "That's your growth area. We're getting three or four calls for every student we can deliver."

At Ohio State, lots of students means lots of clout. With enrollments booming in the sixties and seventies, Agriculture Dean Roy Kottman headed one of the campus power bastions. The pundits said that if he succeeded President Fawcett, he would step down in authority. To the rest of the university, Harold Bauman said, agriculture seemed "a mysterious, rich, politicized subkingdom." Now Bauman was striding across a parking lot, going from his office to the new agricultural engineering building. He waved his arm to sweep in the whole ag campus, the subkingdom. "We are big. All these buildings are ours."

In some ways, the college suffered less than it might have, he said. "While our decrease is fifty percent, the university has been slow to redistribute budgets. But you do need almost the same resources to teach the other half. If we had a hundred percent increase, we'd be right over there in the president's office—'Where's the money? Where's the money?' Right now, we're being quiet."

On the other hand, the college seemed a likely prey to turf vultures. Bauman arrived at the college's brand new building, just opened in early 1987 for agricultural engineering. But that department had thirty-some majors and here was some 85,000 square feet. While departments across the Olentangy were starved for space, this building had thousands of square feet so specialized that they were used infrequently by only a few. Bauman walked along the halls, admiring a new classroom, computers, a lab. "It's neat, it's new," he said. "But there are no secrets in a place like this. People observe your space and they want some. You're always trying to defend turf, but the minute you don't have student numbers it's tough to do right."

To maintain itself—to survive with any heft at all—the college decided it had to increase its urban enrollment. After all, students from agricultural backgrounds were an ever-diminishing resource. So one approach the college came up with was to downplay the word *agriculture*. Kenneth Reisch, an associate dean (with five associates and four assistants, the college abounds in deans—Bauman said, "We have a caste system you wouldn't believe") pulled out the latest College of Agriculture recruiting literature: "Invest in Business," "Specialize in Information," "Discover in Science." "You don't see it's agriculture until you open it up," Reisch explained. "We felt if we could get students aware, then we could invite them to campus for Ag Day." He quickly added that the "Ag" was going to come out of Ag Day. It's already off career information sheets, which used to say "Careers in Agriculture" across the top. "We took that off starting about 1983," Reisch said. "We hired a consultant. Now everything starts with 'You.'"

Reisch has been at OSU since 1952; he spent twenty years in horticulture before becoming a dean. In 1969 he started to keep scrapbooks of clips on agriculture from *The Lantern* and Columbus papers. They included stories on the student who sued OSU after he was bitten by a hog in class, on contact lenses for horses, on a jogger who suffered a heart attack in front of the Ag Administration building. But what Reisch was mostly concerned about now were stories that made agriculture sound too bucolic (headlines about hay or hog wallowing) or too dead-end (as in "Ag courses fading along with family farms"). He liked "Graduates to find bushels of jobs" or "Diversity draws students to careers in agriculture."

Reisch even invited Walter Bunge, who heads the School of Journalism, to come over to see examples of *Lantern* headlines that were giving agriculture a bad image. "I told Bunge, 'We're trying to project a modern scientific image, and you're making us look like we just got out of the barn.' Well, Bunge laughed and said that if he went and told the student editors all this, there would just be a backlash."

Enrollment slumps were not the only sources of change. Another was what Harold Bauman called "recycling of people." The state was encouraging employee retirements with buyouts that gave longtime staff credit for extra years. Agriculture had a large cadre of people who arrived en masse after World War II and stayed en masse. "One of the real hallmarks of this college is its stability," Bauman said. "Some people would say, 'That's one of your problems. Stuck in the mud.'" Now, the postwar arrivals were leaving en masse: Including extension people, about 25 percent of the college's faculty retired in 1986–88. "The average age plunges from sixty, fifty-five, to forty-two," Bauman said.

Bauman himself planned to retire September 1, 1988, even though he still looked forward to coming to work every morning and was not yet sixty-five. So why was he leaving? Everyone else was, he mumbled. "We're flushing out the old and bringing in the new. Very soon a great deal of the memory will be gone. Some would say that's good—you're not fettered." Some departments had a huge turnover. Bill Pope, a new assistant professor in Animal Science, said his department had a one third turnover in two years. "It was probably too fast," he said. "We came in like gangbusters."

And then there was research. From the late nineteenth century, while OSU taught agriculture in Columbus, Ohio Agricultural Research and Development Center (OARDC) at Wooster did the research. "For a long time," says George Johnson, an emeritus who in 1958 began a quarter century as chairman of Animal Science, "this department was recognized for outstanding undergraduate teaching. In the sixties and early seventies, we had such a rapid increase in student numbers that it was difficult to do much research."

The OARDC had its own board until 1981, when it was merged into the university and research began to figure more prominently on the Columbus campus. Then, as Ken Reisch says, in the mid-eighties a vice-president, Max Lennon, "turned the college around in research and biotechnology. Biotechnology was a new tool and Max strengthened it." Biotechnology arrived in both teaching and research, not only at Ohio State but in most agricultural schools.

At Ohio State, which in 1873 began teaching fruit growing, farm hedges, tillage, and animal diseases, the interest in biotechnology seemed to downplay the traditional agriculture. "Many of the new people are not agriculturists," Bauman said. "They're gene manipulators and biological types. Some could have been in another OSU college as far as their credentials are concerned. Is that good or bad? That's the way it is." Now he was touring labs in Vivian Hall. The June morning was hot; his face was flushed.

Bauman had a good peg for the changes in research: Kottman Hall. "It's our next-to-newest building, six years old. Design started in 1976 and provided for very few research or teaching laboratories—the level of sophistication was a sink, water, a few tables and that was about it. That's not to say it wasn't good. But now we're in an eight-hundred-fifty-thousand-dollar lab renovation for a six-year-old building—seventy-five dollars a square foot to remodel a six-year-old building. Have you lost your mind? The old-timer looks at this and says, 'You never spent this much on me. What could I have done if you had?' But the new people have different expectations from the start. The new people want to be respected scientists."

Tim Ramsay was one. In a newly remodeled lab in the Animal Science building, he was doing obesity research that could be applied to animals or people (he said, "A cell is a cell is a cell"). Specifically, he was trying to find out how to grow the low-fat-meat animals that consumers want (he said, "Over a billion dollars is wasted on fat product that's thrown away"). So he was trying to find exactly what makes fat cells grow—or, not grow.

At thirty-one, Ramsay was young for a professor who'd been on the job three years. Because new-breed agricultural scientists were in such demand, he skipped a post-doc interlude when OSU hired him right out of graduate school in 1985. His PhD, though based on research with pigs, is in human nutrition. Now one of fifteen to twenty U.S. scientists trying to reduce meat fat by way of the test tube, he was in a job so new in agriculture that it didn't exist anywhere before 1980. Ramsay wouldn't know how to begin running a farm, and he hoped that students from Biological Sciences would end up taking courses in the College of Agriculture. He said, "It's not just feed 'em and weigh 'em."

Ramsay and Bill Pope, another of the new people, both had fifty-fifty contracts—half teaching, half research. Pope did get out of the lab and into the barn for research in reproduction—"We don't know enough yet to mimic the live uterus in culture." He was trying to improve embryo survival in sheep and swine. "My job," he said, "is to keep food cheap." He averred that if the family farm became uneconomical, "that's fine with me. We don't work for farmers; we work for farming. That's the way I teach: What breeding decisions will lead to more profit? I don't tell students, 'June first you put the bull in with the cows.' Courses used to take a farmer through the seasons like that. Now there are so many changes. I try to give students the knowledge to figure out what to do tomorrow. It's a cold business nowadays."

Actually, Pope said, efficiency-oriented research was what set him and his colleagues apart from zoologists: "We're dealing with species that have economic value." Harold Bauman put it this way: "The things the researchers do will ultimately benefit the corn grower. That's nothing new. It's just the forty-fifth verse of the same song." Over the decades, education and research had made agriculture so efficient that fewer people and less land were enough. That was still going on.

But on the farm, for better and worse, Nature is still a player. For worse, in 1988 no one could stem the devastation from a hot summer with no rain. In mid-August, Craig Fendrick is standing at the edge of a cornfield on west campus. It is the first time ever that Fendrick, who is five feet eight inches tall, has looked down on corn in August.

He recites a litany of the woes that have befallen this crop: "The first effect of the drought is population loss. We lost twenty percent of what we'd normally have. The second thing is, we lost our weed control. It takes rain to activate it." Some of the stunted stalks were entwined with morning glory; others yielded to velvet leaf or Johnson grass.

"Number three, height," Fendrick went on. "We've lost twenty percent of the height. This is five feet tall and it would normally be six or seven feet. Normally we'd be looking right into the ear. But the next thing that happened was ear set. See, we have a number of barren stalks."

The ears that survive are mostly stunted five-inch cobs with a third of the usual kernels. Some ears grow abnormally, in place of the tassel at the top of the stalk. Wilt crinkled leaves; plagues of fungus and smut sickened the weak; insects went after what was left. Finally Fendrick says, "We're fortunate. We've got a crop. We've got sixty percent of silage and half of our corn for grain at London."

Then in the pickup truck, on the way to look at his other cornfields, he talks about the better side: resurgence. The late-summer rains might give him a fourth cutting of hay, which was very unusual. And the soybeans have almost fully recovered. "Our soybeans at London will be reasonably normal, but very late. The beans aborted their first blooms and pods in the drought. With the rain, they set new blooms and new pods. They'll be three weeks late, but we should get ninety percent.

"It's unbelievable."

AUGUST CALENDAR

Bees in the Beard. The second week in August, Sandi Rutkowski was finishing the 1988 *Synergy* magazine. Though she was still waiting for some photographs, she did have a cover picture: Rob Page with a swarm of bees on his hand— they looked like an enormous boxing glove. Rutkowski was pleased with the picture (one of only two that caught Page with his eyes open): "He has bees in his eyebrows and beard and there's one just about to go up his nose. I think it's going to be the best cover I ever had."

Twelve-Year-Olds on Campus. In early August two hundred seventh graders from Ohio cities were living on campus, learning about college. They were part of a program designed to pick talented students from low-income families, start them early on a college track, and guarantee them admission and scholarships. One of their counselors, an OSU senior, said she wished the program had been around in her day. To be sure of an academic scholarship, she'd had to work so hard in high school.

Trash Crashing. Crew coach Jim Brown complained about debris in the Olentangy River. Logs and large chunks of concrete left over from a construction project had damaged one of the crew's boats and several of their two-hundred-dollar oars. The construction company that left the concrete said the real problem was low water. Brown just hoped the crew wouldn't have to start going somewhere else to practice. So long as they weren't crashing trash, they were so lucky to have a river in the middle of campus.

Just Like Earle. After seven months as football coach John Cooper's secretary, Julie Bonfini reported that actually, "He and I work pretty much the same as Earle and I did. He has a certain calmness—Earle was more excitable." In Cooper's first months, Bonfini had booked him for well over a hundred speeches—sometimes, for as many as three a day, one for each meal.

Football Team Picture. Once the players assembled in Columbus, they met on the gray and muggy morning of Friday, August 19, for team pictures in Ohio Stadium. For the picture, they lined up on bleachers, with President Jennings and Athletic Director Jim Jones sitting at the ends of the front row. Next to a 240-pound guard buttressed by shoulder pads, Jennings, who is not a small man, looked runty. While they waited for the photographer to get ready, the players, the gods of autumn, squirmed and giggled like boys.

Later, standing on the field with a football in his hand, Coach Cooper was available for interviews. "If they play hard, that's all I ask them to do," he said to a cluster of microphones under his chin. "What about your quarterback situation?" a reporter asked. "Greg Frey is a good solid athlete," Cooper answered. He went on, avoiding firm promises like a great ball carrier avoids a block: "There's pressure on the coach, on the offense, on the defense . . . I'm not worried about the past . . . Earle Bruce got a lot out of the talent he had here . . . I don't judge on how much they win or lose. I judge on how well they play." Cooper kept the football in his left hand and shook it for emphasis.

Points of View. With the drought relieved but not forgotten, Jeffery Rogers, a climatologist in the Geography Department, took about a dozen phone calls from news organizations asking if the greenhouse effect caused the hot, dry summer: Was the earth cooking because of atmospheric residues from fossil-fuel combustion? Rogers didn't think so. "We've had warm decades before, like the nineteen-thirties. If we got two hot decades in a row, that would be telling evidence. A decade ago, everybody was expecting a colder climate." Meanwhile, all the media talk about the greenhouse effect inspired Donald Miller, chair of nuclear engineering, to point out that the nuclear-energy alternative to fossil fuels was "beginning to look more favorable."

Noisy Night. Rainstorms having resumed, one struck OSU's Lake Erie outpost, Gibraltar Island, at 1:30 A.M. August 15, uprooted fifty trees, and woke up the thirty-five students and faculty in residence at Stone Lab.

Horseshoe-Counting on Campaign Trail. *Lantern* reporter Patricia Kinneer covered an August 20 Ohio State Fair appearance by newly nominated presidential candidate George Bush and his running mate, Dan Quayle. With their jackets off and their shirt sleeves rolled up, the two spent ten minutes pitching horseshoes ("about twenty-five horseshoes across the thirty-foot pit," Kinneer wrote), and then Quayle answered questions about his National Guard service during the Vietnam War.

Winning Splash. An Ohio State senior, Patrick Jeffrey, won a spot on the U.S. men's diving team, which would go to Seoul for the Olympics in September. Jeffrey came from behind in August 21 tryouts in Indianapolis.

The Law School Fraction. On August 22, as the rest of the university began the last week of summer quarter classes, the College of Law started its fall semester. First-year enrollment was 234, of whom 44 percent were women and 9 percent minorities. There had been 1,420 applicants.

Law registrar Lee Mangia said the semester system was

useful for keeping the college in sync with the profession—bar review courses, for example, begin in June—but did set it apart from the rest of the campus. For instance, a paid fee card from law said "winter" all spring. "Sometimes they wouldn't let us play golf," Mangia said. "That's the biggest problem. I advise students that it's a big university and we're a mere fraction and should be tolerant. But sometimes lawyers are intolerant."

As she points out, the law school is self-contained, with all 630 students and their classrooms, library, and registrar in one building. Along a corridor is a display case—WELCOME, CLASS OF 1991—where 234 portraits are on display. A girl, looking at it, complains to a friend, "Oh, mine is so bad." If she stays and graduates—there is a better than 95 percent chance that she will—then after 1991 her picture will be among those on exhibit farther up the hall. There the law school has a display of large, rigid boards hinged like a book, with the pages holding pictures of every member of every class since 1902. By now, it is nearly a century of faces.

News Items. Toward the end of August, construction on the cancer research hospital, which was already two years behind schedule, stopped because of a dispute between the contractor and the state. Three new contractors were asked to submit bids to finish the job.

On the twenty-fifth, the Library for Communication and Graphic Arts celebrated the seventy-fifth birthday of the late cartoonist Walt Kelly, creator of Pogo. The party featured cake, champagne, and lectures.

Wedding. The university put out a two-sentence press release August 25, to announce that President Jennings, whose first marriage had been dissolved in January, would marry OSU Development staffer Barbara Real. Real resigned her job August 31 and the wedding was September 4, a Sunday.

Novel Subject. OSU policeman Larry Johnson sent the (unsolicited) manuscript of his first mystery novel to a New York publisher August 30. On September 1 he started on his second book. This one would be set in a university. He was considering a fictitious name: University of Ohio.

It Takes Everybody—Until Retirement. Harold Bauman, assistant dean of the College of Agriculture, retired effective September 1; before the end of the week, he was painting his garage. In mid-August, Bauman had been feted at two retirement parties. The first one, in Kottman Hall auditorium, was especially large. "Everybody came," he said. "I really did appreciate that." After all, he observed, it takes everybody to run this place.

CHAPTER 12

Alma Mater's Apron Strings

In its first 111 years of graduations—1878–1988—The Ohio State University, by granting some 373,000 degrees to 320,000 individuals, peopled the world with its alumni. Almost 300,000 are now living: enough to inhabit every corner of Ohio, every state of the nation and 140 nations of the world. So far as the university knows (not all alumni report where they are), 1.3 percent of the people in Ohio are OSU graduates; of the state's congressional and state legislators, 22 percent attended Ohio State. California has 12,500 OSU alumni; Florida has 9,700; Michigan, New York, Pennsylvania, and Texas all have more than 5,000. President Jennings has described an alumni meeting in Beijing; he could also meet with groups in Bolivia or Nepal, in Iceland, Ethiopia, or Yugoslavia.

An Ohio State degree is no guarantee of a distinguished career. One graduate, who barely squeaked through, has been mowing county highways for twenty years. And not all Ohio State students who went on to careers of distinction, graduated. Even without their degrees, humorist James Thurber and painter George Bellows gained renown.

At least six Ohio State alumni have garnered the public recognition of being on the cover of *Time* magazine. The six included two military men—World War II Eighth Army commander Robert Eichelberger and former Strategic Air Commander Curtis LeMay. The others were cartoonist Milton Caniff, golfer Jack Nicklaus, Thurber (A SURE GRASP OF CONFUSION, said *Time*), broadcasting executive Fred Silverman, and writer Marabel Morgan. These six covers, framed, hang in the halls of the Alumni House, a wing of the Fawcett Center for Tomorrow. They are not far from seven George Bellows drawings of campus scenes; in another hall are drawings and poems by Caniff. A poem begins: "When first I walked the Oval, frightened, homesick, unprepared;/ It seemed it all began that day . . ."

Ohio State has given two earned degrees and an honorary doctorate to artist Roy Lichtenstein, a founder of Pop Art. It has nurtured Pulitzer Prize winners; inventors (nylon and the automobile self-starter); 1944 vice-presidential candidate John Bricker, who lost with Thomas Dewey. The soul of Indiana, basketball coach Bobby Knight, is an Ohio State graduate. So is the University of Michigan's longtime football coach, Bo Schembechler.

Ohio State can stay in a family, generation after generation. Trustee Shirley Bowser '56 is the granddaughter of an OSU football player, the daughter of two graduates, and the mother of one. In 1960 Marlene Owens, the daughter of alumnus and 1930s track star Jesse Owens, became Ohio State's first black homecoming queen. In the fall of 1987 Jack Nicklaus's son Gary was a freshman. At the end of his first season Gary had the sixth best record of fourteen on the men's golf team.

When Ohio State alumni leave, they remember their alma mater. Forever. Seventy-one years after his graduation, in the spring of 1988, Ralph Sturgeon '17, a retired poultry grower, became a life member of the Alumni Association. At the time, he was ninety-four—not too late to decide that if it weren't for Ohio State, "I'd still be a clodhopper down on the farm." He said that because of his age, the association halved his fee to $250. "I said that was a good bargain."

People who went to OSU become dues-paying members of the Alumni Association at a rate—38.7 percent—exceeded among public institutions only by the Naval Academy and the University of Virginia. Similarly, the total membership of 103,000 is in the top three for sheer numbers. These sometime Buckeyes have joined over two hundred local (such as, Guernsey County; Baltimore, Maryland; Kenya) and special-interest (such as, Architecture, Nursing) clubs. During 1987, Ohio State alumni met somewhere in the world every twenty hours, on average.

The oldest living alumna was Cora Evans, who graduated in 1906 with a major in classics and ancient languages. Late in 1987, when she was 103, she told *Lantern* writer Leah Weaver that today's students were more serious than her contemporaries had been. "I think they realize going to college now is more a matter of preparing to make a living. We were in college mainly to learn and experience." She said that her era was "so very conservative. I was a basketball player—a very poor one at that—and we had to wear skirts over our bloomers when we played. It was a joke." She pointed out another difference: "The Oval was a sacred spot for us. But we didn't 'hang out' there. We 'lounged.'"

Sometimes, alumni leave and then return, so that their lives entwine recurringly with their university. Among those who came back are a Benefactress, a Professor, a Trustee, and a Hero.

Molly Brown Caren '35 is the Benefactress. When she was a student at Ohio State, she was not a conspicuous one. Because she'd grown up on her family's orchard, she did well in botany ("I knew botanical things that pleased the professor"), but she majored in English; honors composition was her favorite course. When she came back forty-five years later, it was again to go to class, though in agriculture. She owned and had to manage two farms; that—and a farmer confounding her with talk of gelds and boars (male pigs, castrated and not)—sent her back to class. A widow in her late sixties, a dignified, citified woman, she suddenly found herself in an arena, one of 130 students studying meat animals. She went on to become the pride of OSU's Program 60, which offers free noncredit courses to people over sixty. It was because of Program 60 that Molly Caren became a Benefactress.

In 1982—two years after she began taking courses; in all she took one a quarter for thirteen quarters—Molly Caren gave Ohio State what lawyers call "a bargain-basement price" on her $2.2 million 992-acre farm near London, west of Columbus: She sold it to the university for $500,000. The difference—$1.7 million—was her gift, and it put her in the big leagues of OSU benefaction. She was following the likes of Ralph Mershon, who in 1952 left Ohio State an eleven-million-dollar bequest; he is the Mershon in Mershon Auditorium. More recently, the big givers have included Wendy's founder David Thomas; the Galbreaths, a family of sportsmen and developers; and of course, Leslie Wexner. The university has a club for donors who have given over one million dollars. It is called the President's Cabinet; but Caren says that unlike the President's Council, whose $100,000 contributors get a party every year, the cabinet has never met.

That is not to say that million-dollar donors have not been properly thanked; Caren and Wexner even attained a certain celebrity on campus. Of her student days, Molly Caren says, "I didn't join a sorority or anything. I was not a big woman on campus. I was rather surprised to find myself in that position fifty years later."

It happened that in the early eighties Ohio State was in the market for a farm. They needed one for the exhibit Craig

Fendrick manages, the annual Farm Science Review, which had outgrown its space near Don Scott Field. To the university, Molly Caren's farm near London looked like an ideal site. It was convenient both to an interstate and U.S. 40; it was near an airport. Moreover it was flat. It provided the vistas necessary for comparing combines at work.

"I didn't offer them this farm," Molly Caren says. "They asked for it." She said no, of course. This farm had been in her family since 1813. But when OSU asked again, she agreed because she had been impressed with her fellow students and their agrarian passions. Childless, she could choose her heirs. For its part, OSU became interested in her family history. University archivist Raimund Goerler wrote an annotated nine-page history of the property and its owners, so that the record would forever be, and would forever be straight.

Most months, Caren visits the London farm, known now as The Ohio State University Molly Caren Agricultural Center. She drives out in her gray Mercedes, which she restrains to a sedate fifty mph; the twenty-four-mile trip from her suburban Bexley house takes three quarters of an hour. She adapts her dress for visiting the farm. Her mauve suit is city clothes, but her shoes are all-terrain, with laces. A net windproofs her hair. Then Fendrick or supervisor Bill George will drive her around, so that she can follow the annual cycle of corn and soybeans. She is interested in drainage and grain storage bins, in deer and birds. She wants to know about the roof on the house, the new drain tile, the brambles along a ditch. Though she was dismayed when the orchard was bulldozed, she has a rule not to interfere. She broke it once. After OSU had occupied the place for several years, she thought the administration building—a metal shed—should be plumbed for toilets, and she mentioned this to President Jennings. The door to the ladies says, THE MOLLY CAREN ROOM.

*   *   *

The Professor is John Peter Minton '58. In 1962, having completed two degrees and a surgery internship, he left Ohio State to spend three years in the U.S. Public Health Service. When he came back, he took two more degrees and joined the faculty in 1969. He is now a Professor in three departments: surgery, microbiology, and zoology. By profession he is a cancer surgeon—a man who, at least sometimes, answers prayers.

Minton has an office in Doan Hall, part of OSU Hospitals, where he is on the seventh floor, between the Hepatobiliary Pancreatic Office and the Surgery Library, near the soiled-linen chute. His office has an anteroom, where his four secretaries (only one on an OSU payroll, he explains) struggle with papers—at the moment, one secretary has stacks of folders spread out on the floor. Minton's own room is small and dark (the curtains drawn in daytime), like a nest where, amid a profusion of possessions (medical journals, luggage, more piles of folders) there is a well-defined place at the desk for the prime tenant. He is a big man, six foot one inch, a onetime football player for the onetime Ohio State University High School. Now he is wearing a doctor's white coat with khaki slacks showing at the bottom. He takes phone calls—a New York physician who referred his niece, a husband who wants to thank him.

When Minton was with the Public Health Service, he worked at the National Cancer Institute in Bethesda, Maryland. "I operated on people who were guaranteed to die," he says. "Could bigger and better operations cure the incurable? The answer was sometimes. That's when I got into this whole thing."

He combats cancer on many fronts, symbolized by all the Ohio State diplomas on his office wall: the 1958 B.S., the

1960 M.D., a 1966 master's in laser cancer research, a 1969 PhD in immunology. "I was the first to talk about laser treatment for cancer," he says. "I was the first to look at chemical markers that meant there was cancer in that patient. With the marker you could get there before the tumor got a real foothold." He has been operating for multiple secondary malignancies of the liver, which were long thought to be hopeless and, he finds, are not necessarily. With an OSU colleague he has been trying to load an enzyme with cancer inhibitors. He has developed a diet that helps breast cancer patients. All this can be a matter of lonely pioneering. "I'm always reminded of Pasteur," Minton says. "When he discovered bacteria, everybody said he was crazy."

Minton came from OSU stock: His mother was an extension home economist on the faculty. He was born in OSU's Starling-Loving Hospital in a delivery assisted by an obstetrician whose brain tumor "I took out thirty or forty years later," he says. "He went back to work." Minton keeps track of what he does. He assumes a prodigious workload which he details in a twenty-page synopsis of what he accomplished in an OSU fiscal year. Thus for 1987–88, he writes, "I personally examined 3,755 patients in the Ohio State University Hospitals Clinic. I admitted 424 patients and operated on 254 inpatients and 626 outpatients." He taught: two or three medical students, an intern and a resident were at his elbow in the clinic and on rounds. He published, adding to his accretion of papers (about two hundred) and chapters. He went to thirtynine meetings on campus (such as, Promotion and Tenure Committee, laser, medical staff) and forty-eight off campus (almost all in Ohio, though one was in Scotland).

Besides, he became one of the Alumni Association's most popular speakers; he was on the road with his talk, "How to Avoid Dying from Cancer Now and Later." One place he appeared was the Williams County Alumni Club in Bryan,

Ohio. "He was one of the best ever," said Dentist Norman Burns afterward. "Cancer surgery. My God, you're talking a pretty pathetic subject. You'd be amazed at the humor he was able to work in." "When people talk about it, they don't stay afraid," Minton says. He started giving his "How to Avoid" talks to an OSU health class at a point where he'd just seen too many advanced cancer cases. It draws two hundred to four hundred undergraduates every spring.

When John Peter Minton talks about maneuvers he's tried against cancer—medicines, chemical markers, operations—he gauges each one by its failures, which were deaths, and its successes, which were more time—years instead of weeks— before dying. "An attorney brought me his wife," he says. "She'd been operated on and was told she'd be dead in two and a half weeks. He came in on a Saturday and sat there in that chair and cried. He didn't want to lose her. I examined her. She looked like a person who wanted to live. Now a large obstruction's been removed. She's going to live. She would be dead now if I hadn't done this. My goal is to see how many additional lifetimes I can give."

Shirley Dunlap Bowser '56 is an alumna who came back as a Trustee. At Board meetings she gives hospital reports—she is one of two trustees also on the hospital board—and sprinkles official proceedings with personal notes. For example, when repairs for St. John Arena are on the agenda, she says that her December 1956, graduating class was the first large group to use the building. Another time she mentions her father, John Dunlap, who preceded her on the OSU board (his term ended in 1977; hers began in 1982). Both Bowser and her father held the board's traditional "farm seat." Representing agriculture suits her in fact (she lives on a farm) and inclination. In September, she is the one who reminds the board to go to the Farm Science Review. And lest they ever forget, she is there to remind them of the land-grant tradition.

As a student at Ohio State, Shirley Dunlap did everything that could have been expected of her. She was active in student government, a member of Mortar Board honorary society and of Kappa Kappa Gamma sorority. "I loved the place," she says. "I made a lot of friends." But she did not linger. She rushed through and got her education degree in three years so she could go home and marry Clifford Bowser, whom she met in high school (the school had fifty students; her freshman class at Ohio State had five thousand), settle down on the Williamsport farm where they still live, and have children (a son and a daughter, now grown).

Before she left Ohio State, she did get to know the trustees, for at that time honors students waited table for them before football games. She was impressed that the trustees came before the game to be served and then had seats from which they could see. "They seemed important—anybody who could get a good seat for a football game must be important. I didn't have any idea what they *did*." Now on the other side, she acknowledges that the board has a certain remoteness—people are always telling her she's the first trustee they've ever met. Sometimes she's asked about high-profile trustees: "What's Dan Galbreath really like?" She sidesteps that, and also the ticket business ("I don't do tickets") and complaints about games. She took no calls after Earle Bruce was fired.

A board term is nine years. New members take seats at the far end of the table and move up every year until they are at the head and themselves the chair for a year. "Your first year is almost overwhelming," Bowser says. "It takes a year just to know the players, the departments, who to go to for help. This is a huge operation." Trustees are not paid, but they do get free football tickets; they have their own box on top of the press box.

A veteran of the Westfall School Board, a librarian who organized several elementary school libraries, Bowser was ecstatic when named to the Ohio State board. She has taken her appointment seriously. She reads—*Lanterns*, clippings, background material, salary comparables; she regularly makes the hour-and-a-quarter drive to campus, where she abhors an unscheduled lunch hour. She asks a lot of questions ("I notice when the answers come everyone is just as interested as I am"). She has explored the institution; when Physical Facilities changed boilers, she was there. At the end of six years on the board, she can recall missing only two meetings. And she always keeps her constituency in mind: "What does the land grant tradition mean for this day and time? I think a lot about that."

The Hero is Archie Griffin '76. Twice, in 1974 and 1975, he was awarded the Heisman Trophy, which goes annually to the nation's best football player. Archie Griffin is the only person ever to win the Heisman Trophy two times. What he says is, "Things good for me started happening." He is not an arrogant man. What he thinks about when he looks back on his college football career, are lost games. "I feel to this day we had a better team than UCLA," he says of the 1976 Rose Bowl. "That one game kept us from winning a national championship. I'd have traded the Heisman Trophy for a national championship."

After Griffin graduated, he played pro football for eight years for the Cincinnati Bengals, and then in 1984 he came back to OSU. "I *loved* being around Ohio State," he explains. Though Griffin looks strong, he is not a big man. He says that in junior high, "they told me I was five-nine. In high school I was five-ten. When I came to college I was five-nine again and when the pros drafted me I was five-seven-and-a-half. That's my height. I had pretty good speed, though: four point five seconds for a forty-yard sprint. I've done some four point four." Now, he jogs during his lunch hour.

An industrial relations major, Griffin spent a year in OSU personnel before moving to the Athletics Department, where by 1987 he was an assistant athletic director involved in the department's massive fund-raising efforts. When the university was in the market for a football coach, he was asked if he were interested in Earle Bruce's job, but he said no. By then he had decided on an administrative track. "I think I could be a coach, and a good one," he says, "but to be right up front, as far as going out and recruiting, going out chasing athletes— that's not for me. Recruiting is time on the road, time away from family. And you've got to keep track of the kids. Seventeen-year-olders tell you one thing and do another. I help. I talk to athletes once they hit campus."

One of the things Archie Griffin does is give speeches— usually at the rate of two or three a week in the fall and spring—he could be out every night if he wanted. "I'm not a long talker," he says. He can go for forty minutes but he's more comfortable at twenty or thirty. He classifies his speeches by the audiences: churches, father-son banquets, service clubs, and business organizations. For each, he has a particular talk: "Church groups usually want to hear about your walk with the Lord, your faith. I give testimony and tie in how the Lord's been good to me through football, and at the end I try to use some scripture." Father-son groups are interested in football experiences. Business groups want football with a motivational message—people who inspired Griffin, such as his parents or Coach Woody Hayes. Service clubs—Rotary, Kiwanis, alumni—want Ohio State, football, the athletics program.

Archie Griffin, like John Minton, was born at a university hospital. As a boy living two miles away in South Linden, he would walk down to campus on football Saturdays and hope for a glimpse of a player. That was before he moved to the east side and played high school football well enough to catch the eye of Woody Hayes, who recruited him. Hayes took Griffin to the Jai Lai, the coach's favorite restaurant, and talked about academic opportunities at Ohio State. Griffin recalls, "Because he only talked about academics and didn't say one thing about football, I began to wonder if he didn't want me to play. He said, 'Archie, if I didn't think you could play for me, I wouldn't be recruiting you.'"

People often tell Archie Griffin that they remember his first game, but probably they are mistaken. They remember his second game, but Griffin remembers his first. The year he was a freshman, 1972, was the first year NCAA rules allowed freshmen to play. Of course, Griffin's goal was to be on the varsity, but people told him he was too small. "It was a challenge," he says. As a freshman, he went onto the scout team, running the opposition plays in practice. The coach said everyone should dress for the first game, but freshmen stayed in their dormitories when the coach, to promote team togetherness, took the varsity to a hotel, to a movie, and then back for cookie, apple, hot chocolate. The next day the varsity met the freshmen at Ohio Stadium.

"In the game, we were beating Iowa. With a couple minutes left in the fourth quarter, Coach Hayes let a couple freshmen in and I thought this was my big opportunity. The first play was a pitch out to me going around the right side. I was thinking what kind of hole would open up—I concentrated on the hole, and with my eyes on the hole, I fumbled the ball. Coach Hayes didn't like fumblers.

"The next week I was still on that scout team, which meant about fifth team tailback. Two weeks later—we had a bye in between—was the North Carolina game, the one everybody remembers as my first game. Well, the varsity went to the hotel and we were at the dorms and met them at the Stadium.

North Carolina went ahead seven to nothing. Halfway through the first quarter, Coach Hayes called for me to go in. I hesitated. I thought he was making a mistake.

"After that I was in a daze. All I remember is that they were calling my plays and I was running the football. It was a great feeling. I didn't expect to get in and then in two and a half quarters I rushed for two hundred thirty-nine yards. A record. And when I came off the field I got a standing ovation from eighty-six thousand people. The first thing I did on the sidelines was thank God. The night before I had prayed to play."

Thanks to the momentum Griffin brought to the offense, Ohio State won that game 29–14. Griffin credits Woody Hayes.

"Coach Hayes knew what he was doing. If I'd known I was going to get in the game, I'd have thought about it all night long and been a nervous wreck."

SUMMER COMMENCEMENT

September 1, 1988

A commencement is a splendid ritual. With costumes, processions, and rhetoric, it signals one of life's watersheds. It smothers in ceremony all the contradictions: elation and fear, end and beginning, tested and untested. For this moment (just as at birth), hope can be untempered; pride in getting here, exhilarating.

Every year, in its four commencements, one for each season, Ohio State graduates more than ten thousand people. At this university, commencements are perpetually being arranged: When one is over, planning begins for the next. It's what Joan Peaks does. Commencements are not all she does, but she is always doing them. She is the one who makes sure there will be a minister, parking for the handicapped, the right number of platform chairs, and a raised flag. ("If it isn't," she says, "everyone notices.")

Ohio State likes to hand each graduate his or her own diploma rather than a blank slip of paper (the university brags about this; not all schools attempt it). So to begin working on the September 1 summer commencement, Joan Peaks collects lists of people likely to graduate. On July 7 she sends the names to Herff Jones, a collegiate printer in Iola, Kansas: an order for 2,078 Ohio State University diplomas, to be printed on eighty-pound art parchment. She specifies how the date should be written out: "The first day of September in the year of our Lord nineteen hundred eighty-eight and of the university, the one hundred nineteenth."

Joan Peaks is assistant director of OSU's Special Events Office, which plans not only commencements but also staff dinners that mark stages: newcomers, awards, retirement. She can handle a request for a strolling banjo player. She knows how to get helium tanks for filling balloons. For Special Events, a crisis is when, after a retirement dinner, the caterer throws the rented table cloths into the trash. They were retrieved from a dump.

"Instructions to the Graduating Class," a brochure, goes out by campus mail. It tells prospective graduates where to buy or rent cap and gown ("Rental orders must be placed by Friday, August 12"), when to rehearse, where to park, to "wear tassel on the left," and what to do if they don't want to attend the ceremony—about a third of them won't. Peaks calls the School of Music for a "Carmen Ohio"—a graduate who can lead in the singing of the anthem. The Carmen Ohio has been a problem recently. In the spring, the girl couldn't decide whether to sing or go for a job interview. The boy before that was working in Las Vegas.

Peaks has to find a minister to give the invocation. "We try to spread it around between Catholic, Jewish, and Protestant," she says. "In spring Rabbi [Alan] Lettofsky's daughter was graduating, so I moved up my Jewish person. I am hoping for an Episcopalian this time. I called, but had to leave word on the answering machine. They haven't called back, so I may have to go to a Baptist." She is talking in late July. She is in the middle of her commencement check list of eighty-seven tasks apportioned by weeks. Joan Peaks, the mastermind of commencements, attended OSU in the sixties, studied social work, and left without her degree. Does she think about finishing, so that one time the party can be *for* her and not merely *by* her? "All the time," she says. "But you're exhausted around here."

Brown boxes full of diplomas arrive from Kansas in mid-August. Each diploma goes in a red leather case which has the university name and seal embossed in gold. Slipped into a white envelope printed with the student's name, it is filed by college, by degree, and by name in a long drawerlike wooden box called a "coffin." Each coffin holds about a hundred diplomas, plus a couple blanks Peaks stuffs in so that, even in case of mix-up, no one will ever leave the platform empty-handed. The blanks contain a note telling the person to go to 320 Lincoln Tower for their own diploma. The coffin for PhDs has five blanks, because they are always indecisive about marching.

Names move on and off the graduation lists during the summer, with the changes printed in-house; some names always come off after final grades. Ultimately, Peaks has seventy-eight name changes (such as "F." instead of "Florence"), 504 drops and 171 adds—including re-adds and re-drops. The five hundred diplomas printed but not used are shredded. Special Events has just acquired a small shredder that sits on a closet floor, overheating on its diploma diet. In the very last days of August, seventy-five diplomas go back to the printer for the addition of honors, distinctions, cum laudes, and summa cum laudes, of which there are sixteen.

Peaks assigns reserved seating for guests of honorees and speakers; her chart is filled with erasures. She proofs programs, catching the typo in Wright Stste, checking the spelling of the first name of Humanities Dean Micheal Riley. She makes sure there will be hooders: doctorates who will drape the loops of fabric over the heads of new doctorates and then fold the scarlet-and-gray lining so it shows. She juggles colleges to be sure both sides of the arena have about the same number of people. As commencement nears, she works late every day.

St. John Arena is transformed for a commencement: Set-up begins Monday for the Thursday morning ceremony. Mostly it is the work of Eric Esswein, head of movers, and a crew of five. They put protective quarter-inch masonite on the floor, cover that with red and gray tarp, and then unfold 1,450 wooden chairs and set them in thirty rows for the graduates. The platform, covered in red carpet, comes out of storage; bunting goes over doors and scoreboards; the first row of the mezzanine is roped off for taking pictures; PhD hoods are set out on two gurneylike tables; and someone brings diplomas over from Special Events. It takes 120 man hours, at least.

But on the morning of September 1, St. John is ready for the Ohio State University's 305th commencement. At 9:27 Richard Hollingsworth, a dean, arrives at the main podium, takes hold of it with both hands, and greets the seven thousand friends and relatives in the seats above. "Approximately seventeen hundred thirty-eight graduates will be granted degrees today, of whom about twelve hundred fifty-seven will be in attendance here," he says. "Of those graduates, two hundred six will receive the Doctor of Philosophy degree; five hundred eighty-five the master's degree, ten professional degrees, and some nine hundred ninety-seven undergraduates degrees in fields of study ranging from Theater to Elementary and Physical Education, Microbiology to Industrial Design. Approximately thirty-eight countries and six continents are represented in this class." Ohio State loves its own numbers.

When Hollingsworth concludes, "And now, with appropriate fanfare, the class of 1988," conductor Craig Kirchhoff takes the cue; his pick-up band of forty students and outside hires begins the processional, Vaughan Williams's *Sine nomine*. From the four corners of the arena, black-robed graduates file in to rows of chairs under banners of basketball glory (such as, BIG TEN CHAMPIONS 1971) and facing the platform where 140 faculty, honorees, trustees, and administrators, including President Jennings, will sit. Joan Peaks, now the veteran manager of a dozen commencements, is dressed up in a print skirt and white jacket. As the processional begins, she pauses to beam proudly. The coffins line up on the floor, at the sides of the platform.

Colleen Bryce Mitchell, assistant minister of St. Stephen's Episcopal Church, offers the invocation: "Oh dear God," she begins, "bless all schools, colleges, and universities, especially, The Ohio State University." The speaker, Frank Hale, vice provost for minority affairs, recalls the day when he got his doctorate in Ohio Stadium in 1955, and as he was being hooded his two-year-old son, watching from the audience, cried, "Daddy's Superman!" In a speech in which anecdotes and allusions flourish, Hale urges the graduates to activism and commitment. Then Trustee Shirley Dunlap Bowser introduces Richard Morrow, an alumnus and oil company executive who receives an honorary doctor of engineering; five photographers rush up to the platform, kneel, and raise up their lenses.

The mass of graduates unfurls into lines, one on the right, one on the left; it takes three seconds for each person to face his college dean and collect a diploma, a handshake, and a smile. In the audience above, people are trying to adjust telescopic lenses, quiet babies, and keep elation from overflowing. Somewhere a horn gives intermittent blasts of acclaim. A telephone operator and cost analyst from Wintersville, Margaret and Henri Albert, watch as their son Brad files up to receive his bachelor's in electrical engineering; he is the last of their three children to earn a degree. The mother, stepfather, husband, mother-in-law, and brother of Kimberly Watson of Columbus, watch as she gets her bachelor's in science education; after the ceremony they will all huddle around her diploma: "Wow. Isn't that beautiful?"

One graduate has WE MADE IT! in gray tape on the back of his gown. Some have come in with leis and balloons; in this presidential campaign year, one has a BUSH sign on his mortar board; other hats say THANKS MOM, DAD, THANKS MARC, and THANK GOD. When the dean hands Laura Drobnich her diploma and says, "Congratulations, Connie," Drobnich knows she is in trouble but doesn't dare to stop. Afterward, she finds the right diploma among the "no-shows" left in a coffin. Overall, though, this commencement goes smoothly. Joan Peaks says, "All the little glitches didn't seem to jump up at me this time."

At 11:29, at the end of a selection, conductor Kirchhoff turns around, sees that only fifteen people are still in line, and does not resume playing. A few minutes later, the band starts again—a vigorous, triumphal recessional. It doesn't take long. Within ten minutes the arena is empty and four men start folding up chairs. By 12:10, the bunting is down, the flags are gone, Eric Esswein is on the platform stacking armchairs. The confetti, the streamers, programs, and champagne bottles are forlorn relics.

It is hard to believe that just moments ago, this same arena resounded again and again with cheers, great roars that seemed to penetrate even steel and concrete and were loudest of all when President Jennings, on conferring degrees by declamation, said, "I congratulate you and welcome you to the company of educated women and men."

EPILOGUE

Beginnings, 1988. On September 15, a Thursday, starting at 8:30 in the morning, Michael Curran, a bespectacled middle-aged dean in a business suit and tie, talks to a group of 222 freshmen who are entering Tne Ohio State University. It is a pep talk of sorts, to impress them with their university. Then the students see a movie that starts in the stars, shows the earth from outer space, and sweeps from celestial heights to a close-up of the campus portals on High Street. The meaning is clear. Though these freshmen will spend this day on mundane chores—placement tests, class registration, obtaining their own plastic-coated OSU IDs—they should remember the ambition of this place.

INDEX

Academic All Big Ten, 144
Academic ranking of universities, 35, 156–57
Acarology, 113–14, 115, 120–25
ACCAD (Advanced Computing Center for the Arts and Design), 99, 103, 106, 108–9
Accounting Hall of Fame, 116
ACT scores for freshmen, 41
Admission requirements, 40–42
Advanced Computing Center for the Arts and Design (ACCAD), 99, 103, 106, 108–9
Aesculus glabra (buckeye), 163
Affirmative action
  fraternity and sorority viewpoints, 17
  Jennings on, 151
Ag Day, 185
Agricultural courses, Morrill Act and, 38–39
Agriculture, College of, 178–90
  changes in, 178–79, 182, 185–86
  enrollment drop in, 182–83
  as independent fiefdom, 153–54
  separateness of, 19
Agriculture, representation, on Board of Trustees, 203–4
Agronomy, enrollment drop in, 183
AIDS Education and Research Committee, 35
Airport, 135–37, 179
Albert, Brad (graduate), 213
Alumni, 196–208
  devotion to OSU, 172–74
  and football, 52

Alumni Association, membership in, 197–98
Animal science, enrollment drop in, 183
Animation in computer graphic art, 101
Antenna Lab, Electrical Engineering, 106
Archinal, Brent (graduate), 45–46
Architecture, School of, and deconstructivism furor, 161
Archives, University, 40, 166–68
Art, computer graphic, 100–101, 106
Artificial turf (AstroTurf), installation of, 54–55
Asher, Herb (professor), 130
Asian students, enrollment of, 70
Athletic Department
  and football revenue, 56–67
  as independent fiefdom, 153–54
Athletic scholarships, football revenue contributions to, 57
Atkinson, Herb (alumnus), ashes in Bricker Hall, 166
Augsburger, Arol (professor), 115–16
Auto thefts on campus, 177

Back-to-the-soil movement (1970s), 183
Baker, William (professor), 145, 146
Band
  at commencement, 212
  marching, 33, 52, 57
Barker, Llyle (professor), 63
Barone, John (trustee), 60
Baroway, Michael (University Communications head), 110
Barron's Profiles of American Colleges,

ranking of OSU admissions, 156–57
Baseball team, 97
Basinger, Mary (secretary), 145–46
Basketball, 81
  women's, 95
Bauman, Harold (agriculture assistant
  dean), 183, 184–85, 186, 195
Bay, Rick (athletic director), 96, 159
  and firing of Coach Bruce, 58–60
Beck, Steven (faculty adviser), 69
Beef, animals raised for, 180–81
Bee Laboratory research, 89
Bees, *Synergy* story on, 140–42, 191
Behavioral Science Lab, as part of Ohio
  Stadium, 53
Bellows, George, 196–97
Bendixen, Leo (professor), 84, 89–90
Bentsen, Lloyd, 177
Berlin Botanical Garden, as source of
  original buckeye, 163, 164–65
Bevis, Howard Landis (past president),
  153
Beytagh, Francis (law dean), 82
Biechele, Jennifer (student), 22–23
Big Ear (radio telescope), 83–84, 92–94
Biology, relationship to philosophy, 176
Biotechnology at OSU, 187
Blacks
  doctorates awarded to, 68–69
  enrollment of, 17, 40, 70
  on faculty, 17
  fraternities and sororities for, 17,
    34–35
Bloch, Erich (NSF head), 160
Bobsled design, 96
Boner Award, 110
Bonfini, Julie (secretary), 66, 192
Bookbags, use of, 72, 74, 76
Borror Laboratory of Bioacoustics, 125
Botoman, Rodica (associate professor),
  44
Bowser, Shirley (trustee), 197, 203–5,
  213
Brand, Myles (provost), 70, 151
Brandt, Willi, 127
Brenemen, David (president,
  Kalamazoo College), 71–72
Breunig, Joe (bus driver), 27
Brown, Jim (crew coach), 191–92
Bruce, Earle (football coach), 33, 57–58,
  148, 192
  firing of, 51, 58–63
  job offers to, 65, 143
  lawsuit filed by, 61–62
Bruder, Bryan (student), 50

Brunson, Caleb (traffic and parking
  manager), 27
BRUTUS (computerized telephone
  registration), 30, 31
Bryan, Ohio, devoted alumni of, 172–74
Buckeye (Ohio state nickname), 163–64
Buckeye (tree species)
  original twig, 163–65
  proposed botanical grove for, 162
Buckeye Basement, 174
Buckeye Grove, 20, 128
Buckeye Room, 174
Buckeye Village (housing complex),
  23–24
Budget sources, 26
Buildings, campus, 19, 21
  history of, 24–25
Building Sullivant's Pyramid (Kinnison),
  153
Bunge, Walter (journalism dean), 186
Burns, Donna (alumna), 174
Burns, Norman (alumnus), 172–74, 203
Burns, Thomas J. (professor), 116
Burson, Jay (basketball player), 81
Bush, George, 127, 193
Business, popularity as major, 42–43
Bus system, 27, 166

Campus Buildings (Herrick), 167
Campuses, regional, 19
Campus Planning, 22–23, 24
Cancer research hospital, 86, 194
Canfield, James (past president), 153
Caniff, Milton, 34, 119–20, 197
Cannon Act (1870), 38
Caren, Molly Brown (alumna), 198–200
"Carmen Ohio" (OSU anthem), 158,
  210
Carter, Cris (football player), 60, 128
Cartoon collection, 120
Casanueva, Maria (PhD candidate),
  123–24
Casto, Deborah (trustee), 50, 61–62, 127
Caswell, Lucy (graphic arts curator),
  119–20
Celebrities, campus protection for,
  27–28
Celebrity Eyewear collection, 115–16
Celeste, Richard, 48, 60
Cell studies, as high-tech agriculture, 179
Center for the Commercial
  Development of Space, 87
Chasser, Anne (merchandise sales
  staffer), 171
Chavez, Cesar, 127

INDEX

Cheerleader costs, 57
Chernesky, Karen (gardener), 129
Chickens, 179, 181
Chinese Scholar and Student Society, 72
CIA recruitment, 51
Circulation Technology, 42
Clark, Bunny (professor), 131–33
Classics courses, 36–38, 222
Cocaine on campus, 177
Cocroft, Kaelyn (student), 35
Commencement
  fall, 65
  spring, 160
  summer, 209–14
  winter, 111–12
Committee work, faculty, 85
Communications Workers of America, 127
"Complex Image Synthesis" (project), 108
Computer graphics research, 98–109
Computers, 30–32. See also Supercomputer
Condoms, sale of, 35, 76
Condon, Bill (furniture warehouse manager), 168
Conference Board of Associated Research Councils, 156
Conrads College Gifts, 177
Conservatism, student, 73, 77
Cooper, John (football coach), 65–66, 81, 127–28, 192
Corn, effect of drought on, 189–90
Corwin, Ronald (professor), 85, 87–88
Costume collection, 114–15
Coulter, William (chancellor, Board of Regents), 86–87
Cranston/Csuri Productions, 109
Crawford, Dan (professor), 165
Cray supercomputer, 31, 48–49, 86, 108–9
Crow, Frank (professor), 108
Csuri, Charles (professor), and artistic computer graphics, 98–109
Curran, Michael (dean), 15, 215
Curriculum, 40, 42–46
Custer, Richard Lyle (Gus), on airport runway maintenance, 135–37

Dairy operations, 179–80
Dairy science, enrollment drop in, 183
Dannelly, Gay (librarian), 29
Davis, James (keeper of student records), 31–32

Davis, John (professor), 36–38, 46–47, 85–86
Davis, Mike (groundskeeper), 23–24
Deconstructivist architecture, 161
De Fanti, Tom (student), 107–8
DeMaria, Sister Jean Dominici, 101–2, 103–4
Dent, Larry (student), 70–71
Diggs, Theresa (Olympic qualifier), 144
Dining halls, 95
Diplomas, handed out at commencement, 209–10, 211
Disinger, John (natural resources acting director), 183–84
Dixon, Robert (radio telescope staffer), 83–84, 92–94
Doctorates, 211, 212
  awarded to black students, 68–69
Don Scott Field (airport), 135–37, 179
Dormitories, 19, 53
Dorset sheep breeding, 137–38
Drainage Hall of fame, 117–18
Drobnich, Laura (student), 214
Drought of 1988, 175, 189–90
Droz-Berrios, Annabell (student), 157–58
Drug offenses, 177
Dryden, John, research on, 84, 90–91
Dukakis, Michael, 177
Dunlap, John (former trustee), 203

Echols, Shirley (artist), 102
Economic development and research, 86–87
Ehman, Jerry (Big Ear volunteer), 93
Eisenman, Peter (architect), 161
Elam, John (lawyer), 62
Electric bill for July 1988, 175
Elevators on main campus, 20
Emerson, Ralph Waldo, 58
Employees, nonteaching, 26
Enarson, Harold (past president), 153
Enarson Years, The (Underwood), 167
Engineering, popularity as major, 42–43
Enrollment, 17, 162
  of Asians, 70
  of blacks, 17, 40, 70
  in College of Agriculture, 17, 182–83, 185
  of Hispanics, 70
  of native Americans, 70
  of women, 40
Esswein, Eric (supervisor of movers), 21–22, 212, 214
Evans, Cora (alumna), 198

Evolution conference, 176
Extraterrestrial life, search for, 83–84, 92–94
Eyeglasses, collection of, 114–115

Faculty
attitude toward president, 149–50
competition and search for, 87–88
summer activity abroad, 162
Farm (OSU), worth as urban real estate, 178
Farm machinery, moving of, 179, 181–82
Farm Science Review, 182, 200, 204
Farm seat on Board of Trustees, 203–4
Fawcett, Novice (past president), 153, 169–70
Fawcett Center for Tomorrow, 153, 169
Fekete, Gene (football player), 104
Fellows, Michael (development officer), 171–72
Fendrick, Craig (farm crops manager), 178, 179–80, 181–82, 189–90, 199–200
Field Museum acarology collection, 122
Fillhart, David (traffic coordinator), 56
Film archives collection of OSU movies, 168–69
used to make football video, 169
Fitzsimons, Kevin (photographer), 139, 141–42, 163
Flag, stolen by students, 34
Flexible-body dynamics in computer graphics art, 101
Flexowriter (computer picture device), 106
Flypaper (computer graphic art), 100
Food-science graduates, 184
Football, 12, 33–34, 52–63, 127, 128, 192. See also Bruce, Earle; Cooper, John; Griffin, Archie; Hayes, Woody
Heisman Trophy winners, 53, 205
1954 season video, 169
1942 team, 33
recruitment of Csuri, 104–5
tickets, 56, 130, 177, 204
Foreign students, enrollment of, 70, 71
4-H Hall of Fame, Ohio, 116–17
Frantz, David (humanities dean), 62
Fraternities, 16–17, 73
Freshmen
orientation, 15–16, 162, 215
return of classes to main campus, 161–62
Fullman, Kim (student), 77–79, 158

Galbreath, John, 54
Gardner, Mary (graduate student), 46, 223
Gay and Lesbian Awareness Week, 144
Gene splicing as high-tech agriculture, 179, 187
Geodetic science, 44–46
Geographic Awareness Week, 51
George, Bill (agricultural center supervisor), 200
Gifts of property, 171–72
Gillen, Herb (student), 177
Giovannini, Joseph (design critic), 161
Glassblowing, 134
Go Bucks (registered trademark), 171
Goerler, Raimund (University Archives head), 39–40, 166–68, 200
Goldreich, Peter (guest lecturer), 34
Golf, women's, 144
Gould, Stephen Jay, 176
Gourman Reports, The (Gourman), 156
Graduate schools
OSU's rank among, 156
Graffiti, 18
Grants, 87
for computer graphic arts, 108–9
Gray, as bus route designation, 166
Greek, courses in
Homeric, 46–47
modern, 112
Greene, Joe (Olympic qualifier), 144
Greenwich Meridian, 80–81
Griffin, Archie (football player), 117, 205–8
Guenther, Ron (shepherd), 137–39, 175–76

Hale, Frank (vice provost), 213
Hall, Tracey (basketball player), 95
Halls of fame, 115, 116–18
Hampshire sheep breeding, 138
Hanes, Andrew (student), 80
Hansford, Jean (campus planner), 182
Harvard University radio telescope, 92–93
Hay costs, 176
Hayes, Rutherford B., 153
Hayes, Woody, 138–39, 169, 172–73
first anniversary of death of, 111
as Griffin's coach, 207–8
influence on coaches Mallory and Bruce, 33
reputation and firing of, 57–58
and sale of stadium sod, 54
Heinlen, Don (Alumni Association), 158

Heisman Trophy, 53, 205
Henthorne, Bill (glassblower), 134–35
Herdt, Peter (police chief), 65
Herrick, John (retiree), 24–25
Hill, John (student), 96–97
Hill, Paul (computer hardware head), 30
Hispanics
  enrollment of, 70
  fraternity for, 17
Histories, official university, 166–67
Hollingsworth, Richard (assistant dean), 157, 212
Homecoming, 34–35
Home-game traffic system, 56
Homeric Greek, 46–47
Homicides, campus, 28
Horse breeding, 181
Horticulture, enrollment in, 183
Horvath, Les (football player), 104
"How to Avoid Dying from Cancer Now and Later" (Minton talk), 202–3
"Hummingbird" (computer graphic film), 100
Hutchinson, Frederick (agricultural administrator), 127, 184
Hysell Act, 40

Ihnat, Bertha (archives reference room head), 167
Immke, Leonard (trustee), 60
Income (OSU), sources of, 26
Industrial Design course, 96
"Instructions to the Graduating Class" (brochure), 210
Insurance Hall of Fame, 117
"Interactive Sound and Visual Systems" (computer art show), 107
International Earth Rotation Service (IERS), 80–81
Introduction to Satellite Geodesy (Mueller), 45
Invocation, commencement, 210
Isolation and Loneliness (performance art work), 97

Jackson, Jesse, 143
James Thurber Reading Room, 119
Japanese language library cataloguer, 129
Jeans, as campus uniform, 72, 76
Jeffrey, Patrick (student), 193
Jennings, Edward (president), 35, 39, 42, 65, 165, 192
  and affirmative action, 17, 82
  at Board of Trustees meeting, 49, 50
  as Boner Award recipient, 110
  dedication of Supercomputer Center, 48
  firing of football coach, 51, 56–63
  as president of OSU, 12–13, 26, 147–58
  and proposed tuition hikes, 143–44
  salary hike for, 159
  at 305th commencement, 213, 214
  on University Inn, 110–11
  wedding announcement, 194
Jewish fraternities and sororities, 17
Job market, for agriculture and natural resources graduates, 183
Jobs, campus, 129–42
Johnson, George (animal science chairman emeritus), 187
Johnson, Larry (deputy police chief), 27–29, 194–95
Johnson, Philip (architect), 160
Johnston, Donald (professor), 121–22, 124
Jones, Charles (Surplus Materials Disposal head), 29–30
Jones, Jim (athletic director), 59, 192
Jordan, Kim (women's basketball coach, Cornell), 95
Journalism Hall of Fame, Ohio, 117

Kanuth, Robert Cranston, 109
Kettering Foundation, 150–51
Kinneer, Patricia (*Lantern* reporter), 193
Kipnis, Jeffrey (assistant professor), 161
Kirchhoff, Craig (band conductor), 212, 214
Klimoski, Richard (professor), 53
Knight, Bobby, 197
Kottman, Roy (agriculture dean), 184
Kottman Hall renovation, 187–88
Kraus, John (radio astronomer), 92
Krebs, Paul (football ticket sales head), 52

Lacrosse, 144
Lambropoulos, Vassilis (professor), 112
Land-grant status, 38–39, 40, 182
  trustee Bowser as reminder of, 204, 205
  and tuition hikes, 71, 143–44
Lantern, The
  annual winter story on tunnels, 21
  on firing of Coach Bruce, 61
  as source material on buildings' histories, 24
  stories on agriculture, 185–86
Larkins Hall, 19–20
Laser treatment for cancer, 202

Latin courses, 37
Law, College of, 82, 193–94
Leafhopper collection, 114
Lennon, Max (vice-president), 187–88, 189
Leugers, Robert (student), 97
Lewis, Richard (alumnus), 34
Libraries, OSU. *See also* Main Library
    acquisitions by, 29
    collections of, 118–20
    reduction in hours, 50
    size of, 15
Library for Communications and Graphic Arts, 119, 194
Lichtenstein, Roy, 105–6, 109
    honorary degree awarded to, 160, 197
Linehan, Thomas (associate director, ACCAD), 107
Liu, Yilu (graduate student), 72
Livestock operations, 179–81, 182
Logan Elm, 20–21, 175
Logos (OSU), use of, 170–71
Loon, Joseph (assistant professor), 45
Louis Nemzer Award, 150
Loyalty Oath, 149
Luke, Susan (student), 145

McCafferty, Stephen (professor), 34
McCracken Power Plant, 80
McCurdy, C. William (acting director, Ohio Supercomputer Center), 48–49
Mager, James (admissions director), 41
Main Library (William Oxley Thompson Library), 11, 49, 153
Main Oval. *See* Oval
Mallory, Bill (Indiana University football coach), 33
Mangia, Lee (law registrar), 193–94
Marijuana offenses, 177
Martin Luther King Day, 81–82
Maurer, A. E. Wallace (professor), 84, 90–91
Mechanic arts, Morrill Act and, 38–39
Medicine, School of
    as independent fiefdom, 153–54
    sale of exams from, 51
Men's Glee Club, 111
Mentors, for black freshmen, 144
Merchandise (OSU), sale of, 170–71
Mershon, Ralph (donor), 199
Mershon Auditorium, 199
Merta, Ed, Jr. (student), 144
Meyer, Anne Marie (student), 50
Miller, Donald (nuclear engineering chair), 193

Miller, Margaret (Greek Affairs coordinator), 17, 73
Miller, Sue (secretary), 73, 76
Minton, John Peter (professor), 201–3
Mirror Lake, 25, 110, 162
Mitchell, Colleen Bryce (minister), 213
Mitchell, Sandra (professor), 176
Mites, research on, 113–14, 120–25
Mitten, Jack (professor), 106
Molly Caren Agricultural Center, 180
Molly Caren Room, 200
Morrill Land Grant College Act. *See* Land-grant status
Morrow, Richard, 213
Mortar Board, 144, 158
Mounts, Scott (student), 127
Moving personnel, 21–22
Mueller, Ivan (geodetic science head), 45, 80–81, 87
Murders, campus, 28
Murphy, James (Building Services head), 73
Murphy, John (hot-dog vendor), 126
Museum of Modern Art, New York
    deconstructivism concept at, 161
    display of Csuri's computer graphics film, 100
Mythology courses, 36–38

Nagy, John (horticulturist), 21, 164, 175
NASA grants, 87, 92
National Register of Historic Places, Ohio Stadium listed on, 54
National Science Foundation, 87
Native Americans, enrollment of, 70
Natural Resources, School of, enrollment drop in, 183–84
Needham, Glen (assistant professor), 121
Neil Farm, 24–25
Newman, Barbara (associate provost), 151
Newman, Melvin (chemist), 88
Nicklaus, Gary (student), 197
Nicklaus, Jack, 117, 197
Nolte, Byron (professor), 117
Noncredit courses for people over sixty, 199

Ohio, laws affecting admissions in, 41
Ohio Agricultural and Mechanical College, 39
Ohio Agricultural Research and Development Center (OARDC), 187
Ohio Sky Search, 92

INDEX

Ohio Stadium, 52, 53–55, 112
Ohio State Herbarium, 164
Ohio State University, The, naming of, 39–40
Olentangy River, 19, 80, 191–92
Oliphant, Jim (student), 50
Olympic trials, 144
Optometry, College of
Celebrity Eyewear collection, 115
Orientation programs for new students, 15–16, 35, 97, 162, 215
O'Roark, Doug (graduate student), 46
Orton, Edward (first president), 39, 152
Orton Geological Museum, 115
Orton Hall, 152
Oval (Main Oval), 25
"mummy" on, 96–97
spring seeding of, 112
Owens, Marlene (student), 197

Page, Robert E., Jr. (assistant professor), 89, 140–42, 191
Palmate leaf, buckeye, 165
Parker, Pat (poet), 144
Parking
at dairy, 180
for football games, 56
on main campus, 27, 81, 149
Parks, Rich (drum major), 144
Peaks, Joan (assistant director, Special Events Office), 209–14
Pedestrian rush-hour traffic, 26
Penzias, Arno (physicist), 111–12
Pharmacy, College of, medicinal greenhouse, 129
Phi Beta Delta, 155
Philosophy, relationship to biology, 176
Photo collection (University Archives), 167
Photography and Cinema Department, 168–69
Pink Floyd concert, 112, 127, 145–46
Police department (OSU), 27–28
Pollard, James (historian), 152
Ponder, Henry (president, Fisk University), 65
Pope, Bill (professor), 179, 186–87, 188–89
Poultry, 179, 181
President's Cabinet, 199
President's Council, 199
President's Undergraduate Leadership Awards dinner, 157–58
Press box (Ohio Stadium), 53
Press Club of Ohio, annual Boner Award of, 110

Price, Gary (student), 61
Procurement, example of, 29
Product Design course, 96
Property gifts, solicitation of, 171–72
Protheroe, William (professor), 149
Public land grants for colleges, 38. *See also* Land-grant status

Qualifications, entrance, 40–42
Quayle, Dan, 193

Race relations, 69–71
Radio revenue, from football games, 56
Radio telescope (Big Ear), 83–84, 92–94
Ramsay, Tim (professor), 188
Ramsey, Dean (Physical Facilities head), 23
Random War (computer graphic art), 100
Rape, campus, 28
Rare Books and Manuscripts collection, 118
Raudseps, J. G. (graduate student), 106
Real, Barbara (development staffer), 61–62, 194
Real estate
as gifts to OSU, 172, 199–200
value of OSU farmland as, 178
"Real-Time Animation Graphics as a Tool for Research" (project title), 108
Records, student, computerization of, 31
Redman, Edmund (chairman, Board of Trustees), 65
Reflectors, radio telescope, 83, 93
Registrar's Office, operation of, 31–32
Reisch, Kenneth (agriculture associate dean), 185–86, 187
Religion, Department of, 42
Research, scope at OSU, 83–94
sources for financing, 86–87
Retirements, effects in College of Agriculture, 186–87
Rightmire, George (past president), 153
Rigid-body dynamics, 101
Riot gates, installation of, 148
Robinson Laboratory, 22–23
Rogers, Jeffery (climatologist), 192–93
Romanian courses, 43–44
Room and board, costs of, 71
Rose, Jennifer (student), 35
ROTC, 73–76
Ruffner, Frederick G., Jr. (gift campaign head), 16
Runways, airport, 135–36

INDEX

Rush week, 16–17
Rutkowski, Sandi (*Synergy* editor), 139–42, 191

St. John Arena, 126–27, 212
Salaries
of Big Ten presidents, 159
faculty averages, 159
for graduates, 42, 43
SAT scores of freshmen, 41
Scarlet, as bus route designation, 166
Schaefer, Jim (student), 50
Scheid, Millie (extension designer), 117–18
Schembechler, Bo (University of Michigan coach), 196
Schlichter, Art (football player), 60
School spirit, 165–66
Scott, Don (alumnus), airport named for, 135
Scott, Madison (secretary, Board of Trustees), 49
Scott, Walter Q. (past president), 167
Script Ohio (marching band maneuver), 33
Seating at commencement, 211–12
Seeds, buckeye, 164, 165
Selective admission, 40–41
Semester system, in College of Law, 193–94
Seventh graders, introduction to OSU campus life, 191
Shaffer, James (computer programmer), 106
Sheep breeding, 137–39
Sheriff, The (Lichtenstein), 105
Silage, 179–80, 182, 190
Sine nomine (Williams), 212
SIT (Surveillance Intercept Team), 28
Skulls, human, dental school's need for, 96, 171
Sloan, Dick (swimming coach), 111
Smith, Charles (Chuck) (grounds maintenance superintendent), 96, 162
Smith, Estus (Kettering Foundation representative), 151
Smith, Forrest (Health Service physician), 175
Snook, James (faculty member), executed for murder, 166
Snow, Carlos (football player), 63
Snyder, Kevin (dairy manager), 180
Snyder, Tom (film archives head), 168–69
Softball, 144

Sororities, 16–17, 73
South African divestment issue, 149–50
Soybeans, 190
Special Events Office, 210
Special Problems Intercept Team (SPIT), 28
Sphinx (honorary society), 158
Spielman, Chris (football player), 128
Sports Hall of Fame (OSU), 117
Spring, Rita (graduate student), 160
Spring, Tom (communications staffer), 160
Star Trek scripts, in library's collection, 118
Stewart, Pat (telephone operator), 130–31
Stinehelfer, Kelly (orientation staffer), 16
Stitzlein, Gary (swineherd), 181
Stuart, Stephanie (student), 16
Student body
profile, 71
size, 11–12, 41
Student organizations, 72–73, 76–78
Students for Peace and Justice, 77–78
Stuessy, Tod (professor), 152, 163, 164–65
Sturgeon, Ralph (alumnus), 197–98
Suffolk sheep breeding, 138
Sullivant, Joseph (trustee), 40
Supercomputer, 31, 48–49, 86, 108–9
Surplus materials, disposal of, 29–30
Surveillance Intercept Team (SIT), 28
"Surviving the Lecherous Professor" (Women's Services discussion), 34
Swain, Marshall (professor), 149–50
Swimming teams, 111
Swine, 179, 181
Symptoms of illness, feigning of, 129
Synergy (annual), 139–42, 191

Tallman, Richard (professor), 42
Tate, Bridgette (Olympic qualifier), 144
Taylor, Jean-Jacques (student), 61
Taylor, Thomas (botanist), 12
Teaford, Hamilton J. (trustee), 60, 81, 110
Telephone Services, complaints to, 96
Telescope, radio (Big Ear), 83–84, 92–94
Television revenue, from football games, 56
Tenure, 85, 89
Thefts, 28
auto, 177

223

INDEX

Thompson, William Oxley (past president), 152–53, 167
Thurber, James, 12, 118–19, 196
Tibbetts, Robert (rare books curator), 118–19
Tiburzio, Terry (student), 46, 47
Tickets, football, 52
  lobbyists' use of, 130
  refunds, 177
  1987 revenue from, 56
  for trustees, 204
Time Machine to the Sixties, 78
Time magazine, OSU graduates on cover of, 196–97
Tolley, Okey (Campus Planning staffer), 22
Tootle, Barbara (presidential aide), 148
Townshend, Norton (early agriculture teacher), 39, 40
Traffic
  on campus, 26, 27
  for football games, 56
  and OSU farm machinery, 179, 181–82
Transcripts, forgery-proofing of, 32
Tree types, on main campus, 20
Trott, Richard (architect), 161
Trustees, Board of, 49, 126–27
  student members of, 81, 112
Tuition, 71, 75, 159
  proposed hikes in, 143–44, 148
Tunnel system on main campus, 21
Tupa, Tom (football player), 128

Undergraduate schools, OSU's ranking among, 156
Undergraduate Student Government (USG), 76–77, 127
Uniform, ROTC, 73–74
University Archives, 40, 166–68
University Hall, memorialization of, 168
University Inn as gift to OSU, 110–11
University Senate meetings, 64
Urban backgrounds, of agricultural students, 183, 185
USG (Undergraduate Student Government), 76–77, 127
U.S. News & World Report, annual school ranking by, 35, 156

Vontsolos, George (student), 111

Ware, Roget (Olympic qualifier), 144
Washington, Joni (telephone operator), 26
Watson, Kimberly (student), 213–14
Weaver, Leah (student), 198
Webster, Richard (associate professor), 43
Wedge, John Christian (professor), 108
Weiche, Le Dale (donor), 138
Welbourn, Warren Calvin, Jr. (Acarology Collection curator), 113–14, 121, 122
Welding engineering, 15, 42
Wesson, Carolyn (dietician), 111
Wexner, Leslie (trustee), 16, 159, 161, 199
Wexner Center for the Visual Arts, 16, 22, 159, 161
Wharton, G. H. (professor emeritus), 122, 124–25
Whicker, George (Physical Facilities employee), 20, 21
White, William (football player), 55–56, 128
Whited, Todd (student), 50–51
Willdenow, Carl Ludwig (German botanist), 163, 164
William Oxley Thompson Library (Main Library), 11, 49, 153
Williams, Gary (basketball coach), 81
Williams County alumni club, 173
Wilson, Curtis (basketball player), 81
Women undergraduates, first at OSU, 40
Woody Hayes Athletic Center, 54, 182
"Wrath of Grapes, The" (Chavez speech), 127
Wrensch, Dana (adjunct professor), 121, 125
Writing awards, 145
Wrobleski, Thomas (student), 73–76

Yellow nutsedge, research on, 84, 89–90
Yi, Gi-Chul (student), 20
Yiamouyiannis, Athena (student), 127
Young, Geoffrey (graduate student), 67–70, 79

Zeise, Teri Perkins (student), 160
Zelinski, Susan (student), 65
Zellman, Scot (student), 76–77, 84–85
Zonak, John (lawyer), 61